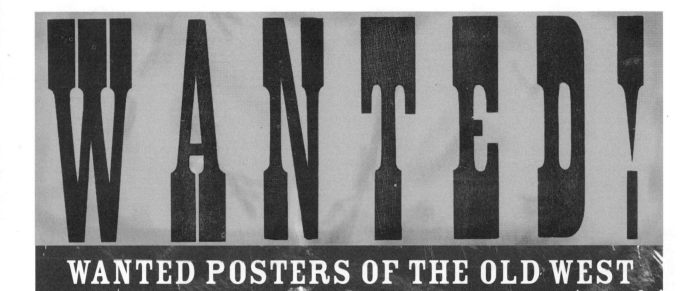

# WANTED!

## WANTED POSTERS OF THE OLD WEST

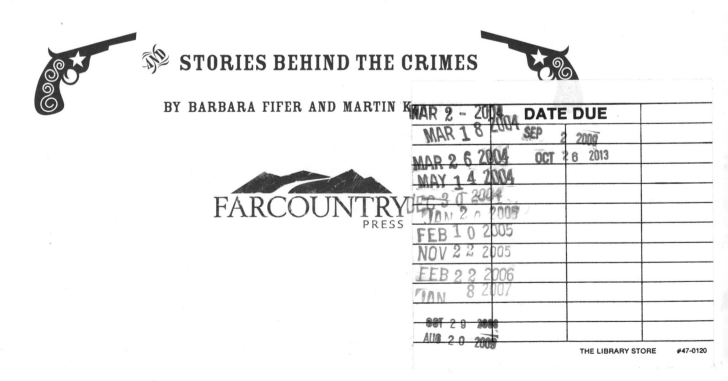

&AND STORIES BEHIND THE CRIMES

BY BARBARA FIFER AND MARTIN KIDSTON

FARCOUNTRY PRESS

ISBN: 1-56037-263-X

© 2003 Farcountry Press

11.97/1 9.95 Ingram

For more information on our books write:
Farcountry Press, P.O. Box 5630, Helena, MT 59604,
call (800) 821-3874, or visit www.farcountrypress.com

466 91     1/2004

Created, produced, and designed in the U.S.A.

Printed in Canada.

# CONTENTS

# PREFACE

A sheriff's deputy was cleaning out the basement of the Missoula County Courthouse one afternoon in the 1970s when he stumbled across a stack of wanted posters dating back to the early 1900s.

The nearly 200 documents, some faded and torn, told stories of murder, theft, cheats, broken promises, and daring escapes.

Intrigued, the deputy showed the posters to Missoula County Sheriff John C. Moe. Being a career lawman, the sheriff took an immediate interest in the newly found material.

"I looked them over and decided they would be of interest to historians," Moe said. "I looked them over and thought, 'Well, I'll put them together in a book.'"

Moe donated the collection to the Historical Museum at Fort Missoula, in Montana, in 2003, and a selection of the documents is presented here. Sources of information for the introduction, chapter openings, and stories are listed in the bibliography.

# INTRODUCTION

———⟶⟵———

## ON THEIR OWN

Early in the twentieth century, every county in the western United States had a sheriff's department and the growing cities had police forces. Each of these law enforcement agencies worked largely alone, covering its turf and doing the best it could without the national data and communications networks so familiar today. Western sheriffs and police departments had to communicate by mail, telegraph, and telephone, spreading the news of wanted fugitives to their known haunts and along likely paths of escape: roads and railway lines.

When they rejected European government in 1776, Americans also rejected a national police force. The only federal officials with arrest power were members of the U.S. Marshals Service, whom the Treasury Department regularly hired after the Civil War to track counterfeiting of the currency that nationally chartered banks produced. The marshals were not immune from state laws, though, and until 1889 states could charge them for imagined or actual "crimes" committed in the line of duty. These officers did not even draw salaries until 1896, but were paid on a fee basis.

When needed, the Justice Department temporarily borrowed agents from the Secret Service—until Congress allowed President Theodore Roosevelt's attorney general, Charles Bonaparte, to create the Justice Department's own Bureau of Investigation in 1908. Two years later the department had thirty-four special agents who could investigate only fraud in land sales or involving national banks or bankruptcy, and antitrust cases, involuntary servitude, and immigrant naturalization.

The Mann Act in 1910 banned transporting women across state lines for immoral purposes, and the bureau seized it to go after criminals who had broken only state laws but traveled out of state with women. The 1919 National Motor Vehicle Theft Act gave Bureau of Investigation agents an additional tool, but it would be sixteen more years until their employer became the Federal Bureau of Investigation. And not until 1934 could the FBI's "G-men"—government men—arrest suspects.

Private industry stepped in to fill the national police void in 1850, when Scottish immigrant Allan Pinkerton founded the Pinkerton National Detective Agency, its logo the "eye that never sleeps." His agents were willing and able to cross jurisdictional boundaries that stopped government agencies. Within five years, the "Pinks" had contracts with several national railroads to protect their lines. Wells Fargo added detectives to its staff in 1852, and the Brink's Armored Car Company came along in 1859. Other private detective agencies popped up, but Pinkerton outweighed them as it opened offices in major cities around the United States and in Canada.

All were ready to go to work when two new types of crime were invented.

At Malden, Massachusetts, in December 1863, Edward Green committed the nation's first armed bank robbery, killing the banker's son in the process. Just before he was hanged for murder in February 1866, Jesse and Frank James and nine sidekicks began the civilian career that continued their Civil War guerrilla tactics: They robbed a bank in Liberty, Missouri. That October, the Reno Brothers lifted $10,000 from a railroad train at Seymour, Indiana. The James Gang discovered train robbery in July 1872, taking a $4,000 shipment of cash along with $600 from passengers' pockets. These new types of robbers all rode horseback until Henry Starr robbed a Harrison, Arkansas, bank in February 1921 and escaped in a stolen Stutz Bearcat automobile.

Both private firms and local law enforcement agencies communicated with wanted "circulars" sent to likely locations, asking for help in capturing and holding fugitives until one of their officers could arrive. Rewards were a hoped-for source of income for deputy sheriffs; the Pinkerton agency and its employees never accepted reward money.

Posters advertising for information about fugitives had been around since the printing press met a literate-enough population. When Louisiana privateer Jean Lafitte was targeted by Governor William Claiborne in 1813, state-printed posters offered $500 for the pirate's capture. (Lafitte patriotically attacked only vessels of U.S. enemies.) Within a week, Lafitte replied with his own posters promising $1,500 for Claiborne's delivery to pirate headquarters on the Gulf of Mexico.

Early posters were printed in small quantities and distributed locally. They listed names but had no pictures—the locals knew what one another looked like. Wanted posters in the Old West were not plastered around as generously as movies show them; as this volume demonstrates, they addressed fellow officers more than the public.

## STATE OF THE ART

The sheriffs and police did their best to create word pictures of the fugitives, but many physical characteristics such as clothing, hair color, or amount of facial hair were easily changed. Officials listed the best details they had on what was not so easy to alter: limps, manner of speaking, and scars. The relative commonness of scars from gunshot wounds mentioned on these posters certainly shows that "career criminal" is a later term for an old type of bad guy.

It was a bonus if the officer could describe the type of honest labor a fugitive might take, as well as the social milieu he would seek, often the company of "sporting" or "lewd" women in saloons or pool halls.

As Europe and then the United States became more mobile via railroads, and cities became more densely populated, law enforcement struggled to invent better ways to identify traveling criminals,

Wanted For
Jail Breaking

as well as law-abiding citizens. Applied science was improving life in many ways, and police officials turned to it. Beginning after the Civil War, photographs, body measurements, and finger-printing became the hot new technologies for criminal identification.

Many of the posters in this book include the mysterious numerals of the Bertillon measurement system and the Henry, Parke, or other fingerprint-sorting systems, and/or rare mug shots.

## Mug Shots

The Pinkerton National Detective Agency claims invention of the photographs now known as mug shots, a close-up of the subject's face from the front paired with one in profile. Other private detective firms and police organizations quickly began keeping these photographic records, but by the 1870s, the Pinkerton collection was the United States' largest. Besides photographing their own captives, Pinkerton agents clipped photographs and articles from local newspapers and forwarded them to headquarters in Chicago. Lawmen who sent the Pinks requests, including eyewitness accounts of crimes and criminals, often received the needed identification in reply.

Getting pictures out to other officials was expensive and time-consuming. Individual prints could be pasted onto a few wanted circulars, but halftone "cuts" for printing many copies could be made only in large cities. Thus, many posters did not include images.

## Bertillon Measurements

Today, biometrics—measuring human beings—is a respectable field of applied science used to design user-friendly buildings, vehicles, appliances, and furniture. Where to place an elevator car's control panel? What's a good height for a drinking fountain? Biometrical statistics provide the guidance.

The field started as anthropometry in the 1880s when Alphonse Bertillon, a French police clerk and son of an anthropologist, invented an application for his father's theory that each human was physically unique, as proved by comparing precise measurements of bony body parts. Unfortunately, Alphonse and followers thought such numbers could identify "criminal types" as well, as if psyches were shaped by skeleton proportions.

What Bertillon's system did, though, was help police get past physical disguises. For about two decades (and many more in France), police around the world thought that collecting these eleven standard measurements was the best way to identify individuals.

The information Bertillon originally recorded on his cards was:

1. Height: in centimeters above one meter (39.37 inches), so that 62 (sometimes written 162, or 1.62 in the U.S.) indicated a height of 1 meter plus 62 centimeters, or about 5' 4".
2. Stretch: from left shoulder to right middle finger when arm is raised
3. Length of torso
4. Span of both outstretched arms
5. Diameter of skull at greatest point
6. Width of skull
7. Length of ear
8. Left foot while subject's entire weight is on it
9. Left middle finger
10. Left little finger
11. Left forearm

A Bertillon card also held mug shots (full face and profile centered on right ear), along with a number assigning eye pigmentation (color plus type) to one of seven classes, a general description, and precise measurements of scars, moles, tattoos or other distinguishing marks, and their positions on the body.

It all seemed scientific and infallible—until 1903 at the twenty-nine-year-old U.S. Disciplinary Barracks at Fort Leavenworth, Kansas. A new prisoner, named Will West, went through Bertillon measuring and the numbers on his card matched those of a man already incarcerated there. That man was William West, who was no relation to Will but who looked like his twin when baffled officers put them side by side. The newer technique of fingerprinting began to seem much more promising. But, as posters in this volume show, Bertillon measurements (or attempts at them) were used for years more in some locales. (Today, Bertillon's work survives in measurements tattooed inside the ears of racing greyhounds, and historic-photograph verifiers sometimes refer to Bertillon's principles when comparing a person photographed at different ages.)

## Fingerprinting

British anthropologist Sir Francis Galton published the first book on fingerprints in 1892. Although he was frustrated in attempting to use them to identify racial characteristics, he had proved that they did not change over a person's lifetime. By Galton's calculation, the odds of two people having identical prints were 1 in 64,000,000,000.

Already familiar with Galton's ongoing work, Argentine police officer Juan Vucetich obtained the first conviction using print evidence that same year of 1892. It was for murder, after a woman killed her two sons, cut her own throat, and claimed an outsider had attacked the family. Vucetich used a bloody print from her home to prove his case.

The year after the Will/William West problem, the prison at Fort Leavenworth began to fingerprint its inmates. That same year, the St. Louis, Missouri, police department was the first city force to adopt dactyloscopy, or fingerprinting. (New York State Police had begun fingerprinting criminals in 1903, the year after the state's Civil

Service Commission had begun fingerprinting its applicants.) By 1907, all branches of the United States military did likewise, and in two more decades fingerprinting was the standard for identification.

The process of visually comparing unidentified fingerprints to those on file was painstaking and slow. Many United States agencies adopted a classification system developed by Sir Edward R. Henry of Scotland Yard, while others chose the less complex one that New York state prison captain James H. Parke and his son Eugene adapted from Henry's. Both were based on the observation that a person can have as many as ten fingerprint patterns, and that "whorls" account for nearly a third of those patterns. Henry assigned values to whorls, depending on which fingers had them:

(1) R. Thumb    (2) R. Index 16    (3) R. Middle 8
(4) R. Ring 8    (5) R. Little 4    (6) L. Thumb
(7) L. Index 2    (8) L. Middle 2    (9) L. Ring 1
(10) L. Little 1

He then added the values of positions 1, 7, 3, 9, and 5. Values of the other five fingers were added together, and the result written as if it were a fraction. Whorls on the right thumb, left middle finger, and left little finger gave a Henry classification number of 18/1, read as "eighteen over one." His system resulted in 1,024 classifications, so figuring the Henry number reduced the search to only 1/1024 of the fingerprints on file.

The Parkes' simplification worked with the prints in the sequence they appeared on the recording card, where the right hand was printed first and the left hand beside it. The Parke system and Henry system "fractions" could match only if a subject had no whorls at all—or one on every finger. Either numeral appeared on wanted posters, depending on the issuing jurisdiction. To complicate matters more, other classification systems were also in use around the U.S. until 1983, when the FBI made its three-year-old computerized fingerprint database available to all law enforcement agencies.

The Department of Justice opened its Bureau of Criminal Identification in 1905 to collect print cards nationally. Two years later, to save money, the collection was sent to Leavenworth, where convicts did the matching. The fourteen-year-old nonprofit International Association of Chiefs of Police soon created a rival print collection—one not reviewed by criminals.

Finally, in 1924, Congress created the FBI's Identification Bureau, its fingerprint files combining those from Leavenworth and from the National Bureau of Crime Identification. Police agencies across the nation sent print cards there, where technicians needed three work-weeks to check a print against the files.

## DOING THEIR BEST

The posters in this volume come from that era of transition, when police and sheriff's departments were trying to enlist science in the service of law enforcement. Personalities on both sides still peek through officialese, as in the description of forger Harry Mays, a "boozer, a dope fiend and an all-around dead-beat." Or Sheriff Aaron Clements' frustration at working long-distance: "Let's all get together and watch this business [horse stealing] closer, and there will not be so much of it." These posters, and the intriguing tales behind them, put a fascinating, transitional era into sharp, living focus.

NOMBRE...................George Parker
ALIAS........"Butch" Cassidy [a] George
Cass............ngerfield.
NACIO..................Americano
OCU...............aquero, tratante
OC................Ladrón de
................caminos, ladrón

ED................años [en 1901]
ES................pies 9 pulgadas
PE................165
CO................Regular
TEZ..................Clara
COLO................Blondo
OJOS................Azules
BIGO................ado, si lo usa
O................cicatri-
................de-
................ar
................ly
................o-
................o,
................do
................le
................ro
................96.

# ROGUES' HALL
# OF INFAMY

**S**ome of the worst criminal gangs of the Old West have been romanticized and rehabilitated by novelists and screenwriters who gave us a sympathetic—even light-hearted—image of the bad guys. It seems that when enough time has passed, nostalgia chooses to admire men who regularly delivered financial hardship, terror, and death. Audiences are shocked and saddened at the end of the film *Butch Cassidy and the Sundance Kid* when the charming "heroes" rush bravely out to certain death. But the truth is much more tawdry: They were suicides. Jesse James was killed by one of his own supposedly loyal men who hoped to collect reward money. Kid Curry was a stone-cold killer, not the lovable reformed con portrayed on television. And Tom Nixon—who knows? Maybe he pretended to forget his nasty past. Maybe he married the mysterious gun moll "Etta Place" and they lived happily ever after in Canada.

This update of a Pinkerton circular later was translated into Spanish and distributed in Argentina, where the outlaws had used the proceeds of this robbery—Cassidy and Sundance's last in the United States—to establish a sheep and cattle ranch in 1902. The header promises portraits, personal descriptions, and criminal histories for each of the suspicious individuals.

As you read their stories, try to transpose the indelible film images of Paul Newman as Butch and Robert Redford as Sundance: Butch Cassidy was the blond and the Sundance Kid had light brown hair. Etta Place's crowning glory was dark auburn.

Cassidy had been born Robert Leroy Parker in 1866, offspring of a Utah Mormon family. A cowboy, he joined Mike Cassidy's rustling gang in Wyoming. When he was nineteen he worked briefly as a butcher in a Green River, Utah, shop rumored to obtain its wares by rustling. Thus the alias Butch Cassidy.

Harry Longabaugh (Longbaugh, Longenbaugh), born in Pennsylvania in 1867, was a boy when his family moved to Colorado. He was a twenty-year-old out-of-work cowhand when he stole a ranch owner's horse, saddle, and gun, was caught, pleaded guilty, and began serving eighteen months in the Sundance, Wyoming, jail. After his release, he wandered to Belle Fourche, South Dakota, where his bragging about prison time garnered the nickname "Sundance Kid."

There he connected with Wild Bunch members George Curry, Kid Curry, Tom O'Day, and Walter Putney, joining them in an 1897 Belle Fourche bank robbery that netted less than $100. O'Day and Putney were caught in town, and a posse got Sundance and the Currys in Montana (Kid Curry was shot through the wrist before running his

wounded horse to death). The robbers were taken to the Deadwood, South Dakota, jail. They escaped, stole horses, and nearly were caught again but got away on foot. By the time they reached the outlaw haven of Hole in the Wall, Wyoming, they had no loot and no horses.

But Sundance met Wild Bunch leader Butch Cassidy and was accepted into the gang.

A deep, V-shaped canyon, Hole in the Wall was both remote and easy to defend. Butch Cassidy used it as a hideout, along with Browns Park and Robbers' Roost in Utah. The gang's success as bank and train robbers lay partially in members' willingness to split up and travel separately after a crime. As this circular shows, Cassidy kept a low enough profile that authorities thought Kid Curry headed the gang.

Cassidy and Sundance partnered for the rest of their lives. By robbing banks and railroads that had the Pinkerton agency on retainer, they earned their own Pinkerton shadow, master of disguise and infiltration Charles Siringo. For four years, the detective followed his prey around the West, even befriending Elfie Landusky Curry, as she called herself after giving birth to Lonny Curry's child. But Elfie had no useful news. The gang ranged as far south as New Mexico and Texas, rustling and sometimes working as ranch hands between robberies.

Used in the Newman–Redford film was the true story of E. C. Woodcock, a loyal Union Pacific railroad employee who refused to open the Overland Flyer's express car for the gang near Wilcox, Wyoming, in 1899. While Kid Curry would have shot Woodcock, Cassidy had the car dynamited, leaving a shaken but uninjured Woodcock—who probably couldn't believe his luck just fourteen months later when he was working in the express car of Union Pacific's No. 3, heading west from Omaha. The train was stopped at Tipton, Wyoming, and here was Cassidy again. This time Woodcock offered no resistance.

To Pinkerton's frustration, Cassidy, Sundance,

# LOS RETRATOS, SEÑAS PERSONALES Y LA HISTORIA CRIMINAL DE CADA UNO DE LOS INDIVIDUOS SOSPECHOSOS, SE DAN Á CONTINUACIÓN.

**HARRY LONGBAUGH.**
Retrato tomado el 21 de Noviembre de 1900.

NOMBRE......Harry Longbaugh, (a) "Kid" Longbaugh, (a) Harry Alonzo, (a) Frank Jones, (a) Frank Body, (a) el "Sundance Kid."

NACIONALIDAD.....sueco-americano..........PROFESION..........Vaquero; tratante

OCUPACIÓN CRIMINAL......Salteador de caminos, ladrón de bancos, de ganado y de caballos.

EDAD..........35 años............... ........ ...........ESTATURA............5 pies 10 pulgadas

PESO.........de 165 á 175 libras.....................CONSTITUCION .....................Buena

OJOS.........Azules ó pardos...... ..... .............COLOR .......................Trigueño claro

BIGOTE Ó BARBA......[si tiene] castaño natural con matiz rojizo.

FACCIONES.........tipo griego......................NARIZ......................Más bien larga

COLOR DEL PELO.. ......castaño, puede habérselo teñido; se peina pompadour.

### ES ESTEVADO Y TIENE LOS PIES MUY SEPARADOS.

OBSERVACIONES. .......Harry Longbaugh estuvo 18 meses cumpliendo sentencia en la cárcel de Sundance, Condado de Cook, Wyoming, cuando era muchacho, por robo de caballos. En Diciembre de 1892, Harry Longbaugh, Bill Madden y Henry Bass asaltaron un tren del Ferrocarril "Great Northern" en Malta, Montana. Bass y Madden fueron juzgados por este crimen y sentenciados á 10 y 14 años de presidio, respectivamente; Lonbaugh se escapó y desde entonces es un prófugo. En 28 de Junio de 1897 y bajo el nombre de Frank Jones, Longbaugh en compañía de Harvy Logan [a] Curry, Tom Day y Walter Putney, tomó parte en el robo de un banco en Belle Fourche, South Dakota. Todos cayeron en manos de la policía, pero Longbaugh y Harvey Logan lograron escaparse de la cárcel de Deadwood, en 31 de Octubre del mismo año. Desde entonces Longbaugh no ha vuelto á estar preso.

**LA ESPOSA DE HARRY LONGBAUGH.**

NOMBRE......... ........................................................ Sra. de Harry Longbaugh

ALIAS.... . .........................................Sra. de Harry A. Place ; Sra. Ethel Place

NACIONALIDAD ..........................................................................Americana

OCUPACIÓN, .................................................................... desconocida

OCUPACIÓN CRIMINAL.........................................................................

EDAD.........de 27 á 28 años [en 1906]...........ESTATURA..........5 pies 5 ó 5 pulgadas

PESO.........de 110 á 115 libras....................CONSTITUCION....................Regular

COLOR.........Trigueña............................COLOR DEL PELO......Castaño oscuro

OBSERVACIONES.........Usa peinado alto formado por un moño enroscado desde la frente.

AL IR Á PRENDER Á CUALQUIERA DE LOS INDIVIDUOS DE ESTA BANDA DE LADRONES, SE RECOMIENDA Á LOS POLICIAS QUE LO INTENTEN QUE ESTEN BIEN REFORZADOS, PERFECTAMENTE ARMADOS, QUE NO SE ARRIESGUEN, PUES DICHOS CRIMINALES RESISTEN TEMERARIAMENTE ANTES DE RENDIRSE, Y NO TITUBEAN EN MATAR SI ES NECESARIO PARA SALVARSE. SON BUENOS TIRADORES, EXPERTOS GINETES, ACOSTUMBRAN Á VIVIR EN LAS LLANURAS Y SON HÁBILES EN LA CRÍA DE GANADO.

Harvey Logan (a) Harvey Curry, (a) "Kid" Curry, (a) Tom Jones, (a) Bob Jones, se escapó el 27 de Junio de 1903 de la cárcel del Condado de Knox, Knoxville, Tenn., E. U. de A., donde estaba esperando á ser trasladado al presidio de Columbus, Ohio, para cumplir la sentencia de 20 años que se le impuso por circular billetes de bancos alterados, robados del carro del "Great Northern Express" en el ferrocarril "Great Northern," el 3 de Julio de 1901, por asaltadores de caminos de los que Logan era el jefe, y los cuales asaltaron dicho tren, contuvieron con armas de fuego á los empleados del tren, saltaron con dinamita la caja de hierro y sacaron de la misma $45,000 en billetes de banco sin firmar, que se llevaron.

## SEÑAS PERSONALES.

NOMBRE.................................................................Harvey Logan
ALIAS......Harvey Curry, "Kid" Curry, Bob Jones, Tom Jones, Bob Nevilles, Robt. Nelson, R. T. Whelan.
RESIDENCIA......Se huyó de la cárcel del Condado, Knoxville, Tenn., el sábado 27 de Junio de 1903.
LUGAR DONDE NACIÓ.........Dodson, Mo...COLOR..... .........................blanco
OCUPACIÓN...........................................................Vaquero, tratante
OCUPACIÓN CRIMINAL.............Asaltador de bancos y trenes, ladrón de caballos y ganado asaltador de caminos y asesino.
EDAD.................................................................38 años [en 1903.]
OJOS OSCUROS.................................Estatura, 5 pies 7½ pulgadas
PESO ........de 145 á 150 libras. ....................CONSTITUCIÓN.........,.........Regular
TEZ..... ......trigueña, atezada.....................NARIZ......Prominente, larga, grande y recta
COLOR DEL PELO....................................................................Negro
BARBA..........afeitada cuando se escapó, pero puede dejarse crecer una barba espesa y bigote de color algo mas claro que el pelo.

ADVERTENCIAS.—Tiene una herida de bala en el brazo derecho, entre la muñeca y el codo; habla despacio; es un poco estevado y de carácter reservado Padece bronquitis aguda, jadea mucho; su estado físico no es del mejor; tiene dos cicatrices en la espalda que parecen proceder de una descarga con perdigones; tiene el hombro izquierdo mucho más bajo que el derecho, á causa de la herida; tiene los brazos más largos que la generalidad de las personas de su estatura; tiene los dedos bastante largos. HARVEY LOGAN también asesinó á Pike Landusky, en Landusky, Montana, el 25 de Diciembre de 1894, y tomó parte en gran número de asaltos y robos, entre ellos el robo del tren del Ferrocarril Unión del Pacífico, en Wilcox, Wyoming, el 2 de Junio de 1899, despues de lo cual la fuerza civil alcanzó á Logan y su banda cerca de Casper, Wyoming, y al tratar de prender á los ladrones, el alguacil mayor, Joseph Hazen, del Condado de Converse, Wyoming fué asesinado.

HARVEY LOGAN.
Retrato tomado en 1900.

NOMBRE.......................George Parker
ALIAS.........."Butch" Cassidy [a] George Cassidy; [a] Ingerfield.
NACIONALIDAD .................Americano
OCUPACIÓN...............Vaquero, tratante
OCUPACIÓN CRIMINAL......Ladrón de bancos y asaltador de caminos, ladrón de ganado y caballos.
EDAD.......................36 años [en 1901]
ESTATURA...................5 pies 9 pulgadas
PESO..................................................165
CONSTITUCIÓN.........................Regular
TEZ.................................................Clara
COLOR DEL PELO.....................Blondo
OJOS......................................... Azules
BIGOTE..........................Leonado, si lo usa
OBSERVACIONES.—Tiene dos cicatrices en la nuca; cicatriz pequeña debajo del ojo izquierdo, pequeño lunar en la pantorrilla. "Butch" Cassidy es conocido como un criminal principalmente en Wyoming, Utah, Idaho, Colorado y Nevada, y ha cumplido sentencia en el presidio del Estado de Wyoming en Laramie por robo, pero fué perdonado el 19 de Enero de 1896.

GEORGE PARKER.
Primer retrato tomado el 15 de Julio de 1894.

432 B

469 R

GEORGE PARKER.
Ultimo retrato tomado el 21 de Noviembre de 1900.

# IN ENGLISH...

The Portraits, Personal Descriptions and Criminal Histories of Each of the Suspicious Individuals, Continued

NAME: Harry Longbaugh, aka "Kid" Longbaugh, aka Harry Alonzo, aka Frank Jones, aka Frank Body, aka the **"Sundance Kid"**
NATIONALITY: Swedish-American
PROFESSION: cowboy; trader
CRIMINAL OCCUPATION: highway robber, bank robber, horse thief and rustler
AGE: 35
HEIGHT: 5' 10"
WEIGHT: 165-175 pounds
CONSTITUTION: good
EYE COLOR: blue or gray-brown
COLOR: light-skinned brunette
MUSTACHE OR BEARD: naturally light brown with reddish tint
FACIAL FEATURES: classical
NOSE: very long
HAIR COLOR: light brown when not dyed; combed in a pompadour
He is bowlegged and holds his feet very far apart.

COMMENTS: When he was a young man, Harry Longbaugh served an 18-month sentence in the Sundance, Cook County, Wyoming jail for horse stealing. In December 1892, Harry Longbaugh, Bill Madden and Henry Bass attacked a Great Northern railroad train at Malta, Montana. Bass and Madden were sentenced to 10 and 14 years in prison, respectively: Longbaugh escaped and since then has been a fugitive. On June 28, 1897, using the name Frank Jones, Longbaugh (in the company of Harvey Logan aka Curry, Tom Day and Walter Putney) took part in robbing a bank in Belle Fourche, South Dakota. All were captured by police, but Longbaugh and Harvey Logan managed to escape from the Deadwood jail on October 31 of that year. Since then Longbaugh has not been captured again.

NAME: Mrs. Harry Longbaugh
ALIAS: **Mrs. Harry A. Place**; Mrs. Ethel Place
NATIONALITY: American
OCCUPATION: unknown
CRIMINAL OCCUPATION: [blank]
AGE: 27 or 28 in 1906
HEIGHT: 5' 5" or 5' 6"
WEIGHT: 110-115 pounds
CONSTITUTION: regular
COLOR: light-skinned brunette
HAIR COLOR: dark auburn

COMMENTS: Wears a high coiffure with a knot toward the front.

When trying to apprehend any of the individuals in the robbery gang, police with that intention are reminded to do so in well-reinforced groups, fully armed, and to take no chances, for it is said that these criminals resist recklessly before surrendering, and do not hesitate to kill if it is necessary to save themselves. They are good marksmen, expert horsemen, accustomed to living out on the plains and are born rustlers.

Harvey Logan aka Harvey Curry, aka "Kid" Curry, aka Tom Jones, aka Bob Jones, escaped on June 27, 1903, from the Knox County jail, Knoxville, Tennessee, U.S.A., where he had been awaiting transfer to the Columbus, Ohio, prison to serve a 20-year sentence for passing damaged banknotes stolen from the Great Northern Express train of the Great Northern railway on July 3, 1901, by highwaymen that Logan led, and who attacked the said train, detaining it using train employees' firearms, cracking the strong box with dynamite, and taking from that box $45,000 in unsigned banknotes, which they carried off.

PERSONAL DESCRIPTION
NAME: Harvey Logan
ALIASES: Harvey Curry, **"Kid" Curry**, Bob Jones, Tom Jones, Bob Nevilles, Robert Nelson, R.T. Whelan
RESIDENCE: Escaped from the county jail in Knoxville, Tennessee, on Saturday, June 27, 1903
BIRTHPLACE: Dodson, Maine
COLOR: white
OCCUPATION: cowboy, trader
CRIMINAL OCCUPATION: Train and bank robber, horse and livestock thief, highway robber and killer
AGE: 38 years (in 1903)
EYE COLOR: dark
HEIGHT: 5' 7 ½"
WEIGHT: 145-150 pounds
CONSTITUTION: normal
COMPLEXION: dark
NOSE: Prominent, long, large, and straight
HAIR COLOR: black
BEARD: Clean-shaven when he escaped, but is able to grow a thick beard and mustache lighter in color than his hair

WARNINGS: He has a gunshot scar on the left arm between the wrist and the elbow; speaks slowly; is a little bow-legged and shy in manner. He suffers from acute bronchitis and often has trouble breathing; his health is not the best; has two buck-shot scars on his back from which pieces of shot sometimes emerge; his left shoulder is much lower than his right one [the picture shows just the opposite] because of that wound; has very long arms for a person of his height; has quite long fingers. Harvey Logan also killed Pike Landusky, in Landusky, Montana, December 25 [actually 27], 1894, and has taken part in a great number of attacks and robberies, among them the Union Pacific train robbery at Wilcox, Wyoming, June 2, 1899, after which a posse chased Logan and his gang to near Casper, Wyoming, and was trying to apprehend the robbers when the sheriff, Joseph [Josiah] Hazen, of Converse County, Wyoming, was killed.

NAME: George Parker
ALIAS: **Butch Cassidy**, aka George Cassidy, aka Ingerfield
NATIONALITY: American
OCCUPATION: cowboy, trader
CRIMINAL OCCUPATION: Bank robber and highwayman, horse and livestock thief
AGE: 36 (in 1901)
HEIGHT: 5' 9"
WEIGHT: 165
CONSTITUTION: normal
COMPLEXION: light
HAIR COLOR: blond
EYE COLOR: blue
MUSTACHE: tawny

COMMENTS: He has two scars on the nape of the neck; a small scar below the left eye, a small mole on one calf. Butch Cassidy is known as a criminal mainly in Wyoming, Utah, Idaho, Colorado, and Nevada, and has completed a sentence in the Wyoming state prison in Laramie for robbery, but was pardoned on January 19, 1896.

and the latter's girlfriend traveled much farther afield than the West. After they had their pictures taken in New York in 1901, Pinkerton agents tried to figure out who the woman was, calling her Ethel, Eva, and Etta. (Researching her 1992 Sundance Kid biography, Donna Ernst found a hotel register signed "Ethel Place" in Pinkerton files.) "Place" was the Sundance Kid's mother's maiden name, and he signed a New York boarding house register as "Mr. and Mrs. Harry Place," making her last name uncertain as well. To date, no one has succeeded in much more than concocting colorful theories about her true identity.

New York was a stopover on the way to Argentina, where the trio—as James Ryan and the Places—bought a 12,000-acre ranch below the Andes. In 1905, after three years of ranching, they began robbing again—two banks, and payrolls headed to remote mines. Etta seems to have returned to the United States in 1907. Fleeing into Bolivia after a 1908 payroll job, Cassidy and Sundance were surrounded by police, badly wounded by gunfire, and committed suicide.

## THE CURRY BROTHERS

Kid Curry was born Harvey Logan in 1867, and his alias of Kid Curry paid homage to Flat Nose George Curry, an early criminal mentor. Two of the Kid's three brothers, Louis and John, also adopted the surname and became Lonny and Johnnie Curry. (The fourth Logan brother, Hank, stuck to the straight and narrow.) Their cousin Robert E. Lee, with whom they'd been raised after their mother died, called himself Bob Curry.

Even though he was soft-spoken, Kid Curry had a murderous temper and was the most violent member of the loose-knit Wild Bunch. He thought murder was the solution when a train robbery met opposition from railroad employees. Butch Cassidy, who saw no need for killing, managed to prevent the deaths of several trainmen and passengers over the time they pulled jobs together.

The Curry boys were already known as robbers and rustlers when they bought a ranch near Landusky, Montana. In 1894, gold miner Powell "Pike" Landusky bumped into Lonny at a local saloon, and let him know that Lonny's attentions to one of Pike's daughters were unwelcome. Kid Curry walked in and began "defending" his brother. After the Kid had nearly beaten Pike to death, the latter managed to pull a gun, but it misfired. The Kid shot him dead. Terrified witnesses told law officers that it was self-defense.

The Curry boys fled to Hole in the Wall, the Wild Bunch's Wyoming hideout. From there, they joined in robbing brothels, banks, trains, and post offices in Wyoming, South Dakota, Montana, and Colorado. By the time of this poster's 1899 Union Pacific robbery, Johnnie had been dead three years, killed by a Montana rancher he and the Kid were threatening for "spying" on them. The Kid was the triggerman who killed well-respected Sheriff Joe Hazen when Hazen's posse nearly captured the Union Pacific robbers.

In 1900, Lonny was killed resisting arrest at his aunt's Missouri home. Bob Curry was in the Wyoming State Prison by then. So Kid Curry was the only Logan who participated in the Wild Bunch's last robbery, a Great Northern train at Wagner, Montana, in June 1901. The take was $65,000.

Kid Curry was arrested in Knoxville, Tennessee, the next year and sentenced to twenty years of hard labor for the Great Northern robbery. He escaped (some say he bribed a Knoxville deputy), returned to Montana, and killed the rancher who had shot Johnnie years before.

In 1904 he and former Wild Bunch members George Kilpatrick and Charlie Howland botched a train robbery at Parachute, Colorado. A posse

Jas. McParland, Ass't Gen'l Sup't Western Division, Denver.

ST. PAUL,    GERMANIA BANK BUILDING.
KANSAS CITY,    522 MAIN STREET.
PORTLAND, ORE.,    MARQUAM BLOCK.
SAN FRANCISCO,    CROCKER BUILDING.
MONTREAL, STREET RAILWAY CHAMBERS.

Attorneys:
SEWARD, GUTHRIE & STEELE,
New York.

REPRESENTING THE AMERICAN BANKERS ASSOCIATION.

CONNECTED BY TELEPHONE.

# $18,000 REWARD.

It has been definitely ascertained who were THREE of the men concerned in the hold-up of the Union Pacific Train at Wilcox, Wyoming, and the robbery of the Pacific Express Co's safe, by the use of dynamite, early on the morning of Friday, June 2nd, 1899. The parties committing this robbery were also guilty of the MURDER of Sheriff Josiah Hazen, of Converse County, Wyoming (near Casper) on the afternoon of Sunday June 4th. Sheriff Hazen at the time of his death was leading a pursuing posse.

The following are the names and discription of

## THREE OF THE ROBBERS.

LOUIS CURRY, alias LONNY CURRY. Age 28 years, height five feet seven inches, weight 155 pounds (about), build, slender; hair, dark brown, thin and curly; eyes, hazel and slightly sunken; nose thin, long and slightly turned up at end; mustache, dark brown, small and curly at ends; scar over the right eye, is not noticeable except on close inspection; wears a No. 8 shoe.

HARVEY CURRY alias KID CURRY. Age 34 years; height five feet nine inches; weight 170 to 180 pounds; build, heavy; hair, dark brown, and straight, usually wears it cut short; nose, prominent, long and straight; mustache, dark brown, and medium size; talks slow; is very quiet; is a good horseman.

R. E. Curry, alias Bob Curry, alias Bob Lee. Age 36 years; height five feet nine inches; weight 175 to 180 pounds; build strong well proportioned and heavy; shoulders round; eyes, hazel; hair, black thick and straight; mustache, black, heavy and hides mouth even when smiling; hands, indicate work; fingers short and thick; nose small, broad and flat at norstrils, looks like negroes· face full, round and somewhat "dished" ( i. e. if rule was laid on face it would about touch the forehead, nose and chin). Has a bull dog expression of countenance, but not unpleasant; front view, rather good looking. Has small bunch of hair, like a mole, at base of nose on left cheek. Wore flannel shirt, and soft hat pulled down over right eye. Wore gold cuff buttons with initials: "T. M." on them. Louis and Harvey Curry are brothers.

R. E. Curry has passed as a brother of Louis Curry. He is supposed to be related, but is not a brother. His right name is not positively known, it may be Robt. Lee.

Louis Curry was proprietor of "The Club" saloon at Harlem, Choteau County, Montana, until January 6th, 1900, when he and his supposed relative, Bob. Curry, finding they were suspected of this robbery, left Harlem well mounted and heavily armed. It is surmised they will eventually join Harvey Curry. When leaving they had in their possession a part of the $3,400.00 UNSIGNED CURRENCY of the First National Bank of Portland, Oregon, which was stolen at the time of the robbery and is described fully below.

A part of this currency consisting of TWENTY $100.00 BILLS and TWO $20.00 BILLS ARE MUTILATED, THE LOWER RIGHT HAND CORNER HAVING BEEN BLOWN OFF IN THE EXPLOSION.

The following is the full description of the money

| Bank numbers in lower left hand corner | | | | Treasury numbers in upper right hand corner. | |
|---|---|---|---|---|---|
| 22 | $ 50 notes, | A3705 to A3726 | inclusive. | A744372 to A744393 | inclusive. |
| 22 | $100 " | A3705 to A3726 | " | A744372 to A744393 | " |
| 2 | $ 20 " | A5641 to A5642 | " | T130922 to T130923 | " |
| 2 | $ 10 " | A5641 to A5642 | " | T130922 to T130923 | " |
| 2 | $ 10 " | B5641 to B5642 | " | T130922 to T130923 | " |
| 2 | $ 10 " | C5641 to C5642 | " | T130922 to T130923 | " |

Banks receiving this circular are earnestly requested to be on the lookout for the above described money.

There may have been five or six men in this robbery.

The Union Pacific Railroad Company and the Pacific Express Company have jointly offered $2,000.00 reward for the arrest of either of the robbers. This means for their detention and surrender to an officer duly authorized to receive them on behalf of the State of Wyoming, or in case either of the robbers should be killed in attempting their capture, the reward would hold good.

The United States Government has also offered an additional reward of $1,000.00 for each of the robbers.

The photograph on this circular of Louis Curry, is a fairly good picture of him.

Parties furnishing information leading to the arrest of either of the robbers will share in the reward.

Information sent to the undersigned, or to either of the above listed offices by telegraph or mail, will receive prompt attention.

Or
J. C. FRASER, Resident Supt.
February 23, 1900.

## PINKERTON'S NATIONAL DETECTIVE AGENCY,
### ROOM 219 OPERA HOUSE BLOCK, DENVER, COLO.

# Pinkerton's National Detective Agency

#### FOUNDED BY ALLAN PINKERTON, 1850.

ROBT. A. PINKERTON, New York,
WM. A. PINKERTON, Chicago.
} Principals.

GEO. D. BANGS, General Manager, New York.
ALLAN PINKERTON, Asst. General Manager, New York.

JOHN CORNISH, Gen'l Sup't., Eastern Division, New York.
EDWARD S. GAYLOR, Gen'l Sup't., Middle Division, Chicago.
JAMES McPARLAND, Gen'l Sup't., Western Division, Denver.

Attorneys.—GUTHRIE, CRAVATH & HENDERSON, New York.

TELEPHONE CONNECTION.

REPRESENTATIVES OF THE AMERICAN BANKERS ASSOCIATION.

### OFFICES.

CHICAGO, 201 FIFTH AVENUE. J. H. SCHUMACHER, Sup't.
NEW YORK. 57 BROADWAY.
BOSTON, . 30 COURT STREET.
PHILADELPHIA, 441 CHESTNUT STREET.
MONTREAL, MERCHANTS BANK BUILDING.
ST. PAUL, GERMANIA BANK BUILDING.
ST. LOUIS, WAINWRIGHT BUILDING.
KANSAS CITY, 622 MAIN STREET.
DENVER, OPERA HOUSE BLOCK.
PORTLAND, ORE. MARQUAM BLOCK.
SEATTLE, WASH. BAILEY BLOCK.
SAN FRANCISCO, CROCKER BUILDING.

## INFORMATION CIRCULAR No. 3.

# $5,000 REWARD.

### PHOTOGRAPH OF HARVEY LOGAN.

The above is the aggregate amount of reward offered by the GREAT NORTHERN EXPRESS CO. for the arrest and identification of the four men implicated in the robbery of the Great Northern Railway Express train No. 3 near Wagner, Mont., July 3, 1901. A proportionate amount will be paid for one, two or more, and **$500 Additional for each Conviction.**

Under date of Aug. 5th, 1901, we issued a circular bearing a picture of **HARVEY LOGAN** showing him with a full beard, making it difficult to identify. We herewith present a later and better picture of him which has been identified in Nashville, Tenn., as a good likeness of the companion of a woman arrested there for attempting to exchange some of the stolen currency.

#### DESCRIPTION.

**Name, HARVEY LOGAN.**
**Alias** Harvey Curry, "Kid" Curry, Bob Jones, Tom Jones, Bob Nevilles, Robert Nelson and R. T. Whalen.
**Residence,** last known, Landusky and Harlem, Montana.
**Nativity,** Dodson, Mo.     **Color,** white.
**Occupation,** cowboy, rustler.     **Criminal Occupation,** Bank rob-
**Age,** 36 years (1901).        ber, train robber, horse and
**Eyes,** dark.                cattle thief, rustler, "hold up"
**Height,** 5 feet, 7½ inches,     and murderer.
**Weight,** 145 to 160 lbs.       **Build,** medium.
**Complexion,** dark, swarthy,
**Nose,** prominent, large, long and straight.
**Color of Hair,** dark brown, darker than mustache.
**Style of Beard,** can raise heavy beard and mustache, color some-
what lighter than hair.
**Marks,** has gun-shot wound on wrist, talks slowly, is of quiet
reserved manner.

On Oct. 27th, 1901, a man believed to be GEORGE PARKER, alias Butch Cassidy, whose photograph and description appeared in our circular of Aug. 5th, 1901, attempted to pass one of the $20 bills of the stolen currency at a Nashville store. He escaped from officers after a severe struggle.

On the night of Nov. 5th, 1901, the St. Louis Police arrested Harry Longbaugh, alias Harry Alonzo, one of the train robbers, after he had passed four of the stolen bills at a PAWNSHOP A female companion was also arrested. They had in their possession about $7,000 of the stolen notes,

**Officers attempting to arrest these men are warned that they are desperadoes, always carry firearms and do not hesitate to use them when their liberty is endangered.**

Send all information promptly to the undersigned to the nearest office listed at the head of circular, using telegraph if necessary.

PINKERTON'S NATIONAL DETECTIVE AGENCY.

OR    WM. A. PINKERTON, 199-201 Fifth Avenue, Chicago, Ills.

CHICAGO, ILL., NOVEMBER 8, 1901.

tracked the robbers for several days before closing in. A gun battle ensued, with more than 200 shots fired, and the Kid was hit in both lungs and one arm. He held off the posse so that his pals could escape, then shot himself in the head.

## THE JAMES GANG

By the time this poster (page 20) appeared, the James gang had been in business for fifteen years, and robbing trains for the past nine. In ten different states, they had knocked over twelve banks, seven trains, four stagecoaches, a fair in Kansas City, Missouri, and a government paymaster at Mammoth Cave, Kentucky. They had also killed eleven people in the course of stealing well beyond $200,000 and unknown quantities of jewelry. Three gang members had been killed by law officers (one by Pinkertons), and two by other gang members.

The Glendale robbery mentioned here netted $6,000, and the Winston robbery only $1,000, with two victims killed.

But the end was near. The gang's last robbery—a train in Missouri—was on September 23, 1881, less than two months after this poster was issued.

Forty-two men had ridden in the gang over the years, including the core group consisting of brothers Jesse Woodson James and Alexander Franklin James and brothers Coleman, James Henry, John, and Robert Ewing Younger.

As a result of this poster, another pair of brothers and gang members—Charles and Robert Ford—killed Jesse on April 3, 1883, with Robert pulling the trigger at Jesse's back just after the Fords had eaten breakfast with Jesse in his St. Joseph, Missouri, home. The Fords turned themselves in to law enforcement, were convicted of murder, and were immediately pardoned by Missouri's governor. They never received the $5,000 reward.

## TOM NIXON

Here is a wanted poster (page 21) that failed: Tom Nixon, said to have run to Canada, was never caught. Maybe he used his share of the loot to go straight.

Nixon was part of the Sam Bass gang, six men who committed the first robbery of a Union Pacific train, at Big Springs, Nebraska, the event mentioned in this poster. Bass and his boys were former cowboys, failed freighters, and laborers who had robbed the Deadwood, South Dakota, stagecoach seven times and gained little money. Then they got the idea to go upscale.

This 1877 hit was their most lucrative ever, netting $60,000 in new gold pieces and currency en route to New York from the San Francisco mint, plus $1,300 and four gold watches from passengers. The gang divided its take and split up.

Back in Texas, Bass formed a new gang and knocked off four more trains the following spring, but proceeds averaged only $400 per crime. The Bass gang was on its way to rob a Round Rock, Texas, bank the following July when Texas Rangers caught up with them and shot the leader. Bass died two days later on his twenty-seventh birthday, July 21. He'd been turned in by a gang member.

# PROCLAMATION
## OF THE
## GOVERNOR OF MISSOURI!

# REWARDS
## FOR THE ARREST OF
# Express and Train Robbers.

### STATE OF MISSOURI,
#### EXECUTIVE DEPARTMENT.

WHEREAS, It has been made known to me, as the Governor of the State of Missouri, that certain parties, whose names are to me unknown, have confederated and banded themselves together for the purpose of committing robberies and other depredations within this State; and

WHEREAS, Said parties did, on or about the Eighth day of October, 1879, stop a train near Glendale, in the county of Jackson, in said State, and, with force and violence, take, steal and carry away the money and other express matter being carried thereon; and

WHEREAS, On the fifteenth day of July, 1881, said parties and their confederates did stop a train upon the line of the Chicago, Rock Island and Pacific Railroad, near Winston, in the County of Daviess, in said State, and, with force and violence, take, steal, and carry away the money and other express matter being carried thereon; and, in perpetration of the robbery law aforesaid, the parties engaged therein did kill and murder one WILLIAM WESTFALL, the conductor of the train, together with one JOHN McCULLOCH, who was at the time in the employ of said company, then on said train; and

WHEREAS, FRANK JAMES and JESSE W. JAMES stand indicted in the Circuit Court of said Daviess County, for the murder of JOHN W. SHEETS, and the parties engaged in the robberies and murders aforesaid have fled from justice and have absconded and secreted themselves:

NOW, THEREFORE, in consideration of the premises, and in lieu of all other rewards heretofore offered for the arrest or conviction of the parties aforesaid, or either of them, by any person or corporation, I, THOMAS T. CRITTENDEN, Governor of the State of Missouri, do hereby offer a reward of five thousand dollars ($5,000.00) for the arrest and conviction of each person participating in either of the robberies or murders aforesaid, excepting the said FRANK JAMES and JESSE W. JAMES; and for the arrest and delivery of said

## FRANK JAMES and JESSE W. JAMES,

and each or either of them, to the sheriff of said Daviess County, I hereby offer a reward of five thousand dollars, ($5,000.00,) and for the conviction of either of the parties last aforesaid of participation in either of the murders or robberies above mentioned, I hereby offer a further reward of five thousand dollars, ($5,000.00.)

IN TESTIMONY WHEREOF, I have hereunto set my hand and caused to be affixed the Great Seal of the State of Missouri. Done

[SEAL.]          at the City of Jefferson on this 28th day of July, A. D. 1881.

### THOS. T. CRITTENDEN.

By the Governor:
MICH'L K. McGRATH, Sec'y of State.

NIXON & FARNHAM, STATE PRINTERS, JEFFERSON CITY, MO.

# $1,000 Reward!

## WE WILL PAY FIVE HUNDRED DOLLARS FOR THE
## Arrest and Detention
### UNTIL HE CAN BE REACHED, OF

# Tom Nixon,

Alias TOM BARNES, five feet seven or eight inches high, 145 to 150 lbs. weight, 25 years of age, blue-gray eyes, light hair and whiskers; beard not heavy or long; mustache older and longer than beard. He is a blacksmith, and worked at that trade in the Black Hills, last summer; has friends in Minnesota and Indiana. He was one of the robbers of the Union Pacific Train, at Big Springs, Nebraska, on September 18, 1877.

He had about $10,000 in $20 Gold pieces of the stolen money in his possession, of the coinage of the San Francisco Mint of 1877. The above reward will be paid for his arrest and detention, and 10 per cent. of all moneys recovered; previous rewards as regards him are withdrawn.

ANY INFORMATION LEADING TO HIS APPREHENSION WILL BE REWARDED. Address,

**ALLAN PINKERTON,**
CHICAGO, ILLINOIS.
191 and 193 Fifth Avenue,

Or, **E. M. MORSMAN,**
OMAHA, NEBRASKA.
Supt. U. P. R. R. Express,

# WANTED FOR
# HORSE STEALING
## ERNEST WILLIAMS

Nativity, Id... ...ht, 146 pounds
Occupat... ...n, Light
Crim... ...Regular
Ag... ...Dark Blonde
H...

H... ...25.5
C... ...d. F. ...11.1
... ...t F. ...8.4
Tru... ...orearm ...45.7

... ...January 8th,
1915, and ... ...ning or Monta-
na. He is a c... ...and will probably seek
this kind of ... ...onvict from the Nevada
State Peniten... ...ently released from that
institution.

The ab... ...ood likeness of Williams,
but when ... ...ing a moustache which
no do... ...ake identification
... ...se and I
... ...ember,
... ...iff.

## Horse Stealing, Cattle Stealing, Auto Theft

# GET ON THAT PONY AND RIDE

Steal a man's horses and you've stopped him from working, getting to town for store-bought necessities, or running for the doctor when the babies catch diphtheria. You've endangered his whole family. Steal a small ranch's cattle and you've pushed a family further from survival next season. They won't even have a chance to choose between cash crop and beef on the table. On the open range, a cowboy stranded miles from anywhere without his horse faces death by dehydration, starvation, animal attack, or snakebite—not to mention humiliation.

These crimes were serious far beyond the livestock's dollar values, even in the days when internal combustion machines were beginning to show up on Western ranches. Hanging once had been thought to fit the crime, but in the early 1900s the punishment was more humane: fifteen or so years in prison. As for stealing automobiles, that was still something of a Robin Hood venture—taking a luxury item from the rich.

# $50.00 Reward
# William R. Dickinson

About 5 feet, 7 inches tall. Weight 150 pounds. Brown hair and brown eyes. Walks with his head down. This picture was taken at the Reformatory at Golden, Colorado, about 4 years ago. He is now about 22 years old. Now his face looks a little older and sharper. I hold warrant charging horse stealing.

Lander, Wyo., Jan. 5, 1914.

William G. Johnson,
Sheriff Fremont County, Wyoming.

# $25.00
*June 5, 1914*
# REWARD

For the arrest of one John Hoge, about 5 ft. 6, dark complexion, dark eyes and hair, about one week's growth of beard. 24 years old. End of right thumb off. Wore tan shoes, dark suit of clothes and black hat. Wanted for breaking jail and stealing horses. Notify

Geo. Shively, Sheriff

Cando, - North Dakota.

# WANTED

## For Horse Stealing and Forgery

This picture is said to be a good likeness of G. F. Chaney who is wanted in this county for horse stealing and forgery. He is described as follows: Thirty-five to forty years of age; dark complexioned, dark hair and eyes; about six feet in height; weight about 190 to 200 pounds, and has what appears to be very large bunions on each of his feet, so large that his feet appear to be deformed. That portion of his shoes from the first joint of the big toe to the end of shoe always showing flat.

This man says that he worked at Warden, Washington last year. He was engaged in herding cattle in this county and will probably seek the same kind of employment. He also works on ranches.

He ran away with a married woman and stole two horses to make his getaway, and before leaving forged two checks for forty-five dollars each and cashed them. He was located at Cheney, but in some way evaded the officers there and is believed to be somewhere in the Big Bend country.

If located arrest and wire this office collect.

HOWARD GARRISON, Sheriff.

Ellensburg, Washington.

# Wanted for Horse Stealing.

*Aug. 29, 1915*

---

Ed. Smith, Alias Nervy Smith, Alias "Nervy". Age 20 to 23. Height 5 ft. 8 to 9 in., Slim build, Weight 140 to 150, Dark Complexion, Black Hair.

Wore wide brimmed Stetson Hat with high crown, and when last seen had on badly worn pair of shoes.

The last trace we had of this man was on August 16th when he purchased a ticket from Wells, Nevada, to Ogden, Utah. He is a bronco-buster, cow-puncher, and sometimes does trick riding to pick up a little money. Will sure look for a job with some cow or horse outfit.

If located, arrest and hold as we have warrant, or any information you may have that will assist in locating this man please forward at our expense, as we want him badly.

FRANK M. KENDALL, Sheriff,
Twin Falls, Idaho.

# $1000.00 REWARD

## FOR

# George Francis alias Long George

George Francis was convicted of horse stealing Feb. 28th, 1918, in the district court at Havre, Hill County, Montana. He is now a fugitive from justice.

$500 reward is offered by the County Commissioners of Hill County and $500 by the State of Montana for his arrest and detention in any jail in the United States or Canada. The above reward will also be paid for any definite and reliable information furnished the Chief Stock Inspector of the State of Montana, that will be the immediate, absolute and sole cause of George Francis' apprehension.

## DESCRIPTION

Age, 45; Height, about 6 feet 5 or 6 inches; weight about 180 to 190 pounds. build slender; light complexion; light hair; blue eyes; good even teeth; deep dimples in cheeks when smiling; smooth shaven. Has web skin between fingers on left hand; deformed finger nails on same hand; right leg has been broken; wears slightly longer heel on right shoe or boot. George Francis has lived in Montana for over 25 years. He has relatives in Mackay and Pocatello, Idaho, and Butte, Montana. He is an old time cowboy, good rider, roper, bulldogger and all around horseman.

He was president of the Havre Stampede Association, and is well known among stampede and Roundup followers. Canadian, Montana, Idaho, Nevada, Arizona, California and New Mexico officers are requested to be especially vigilant.

Any information given will be discreetly investigated and treated strictly confidential.

Write, telephone or wire

### FRANK C. LAVIGNE
#### Chief Stock Inspector

State Capitol            3            Helena, Montana

# THE LONE DEATH OF LONG GEORGE FRANCIS

by ELIZABETH CHENEY

A TALL and imposing cowboy named Long George Francis—a mixture of good and bad in the classic Robin Hood pattern—has become a legendary figure in Northern Montana's Highline country. His love for fancy dress and for a country "schoolmarm" brought him to lonely death in a Montana blizzard 46 years ago this winter.

Long George Francis was, in fact, known as the "Robin Hood of the Highline." The Highline, so-called by Montanans, is the mainline of the Great Northern Railroad which James J. Hill rushed across Northern Montana in the late 1880's.

Little is known of the early life of Long George except that he was born in Idaho and spent his childhood with his father, a rancher and trapper on the Shoshone River. Long George often said that he had learned to ride a horse when he was six and had since felt more at home in the saddle than any other place. To this early training he probably owed his fame as a rider and roper—"one of the best in the United States," according to the Havre Plaindealer of September 30, 1918.

At the age of sixteen, Long George, who by this time had stretched out to a height of six feet six inches, helped drive a herd of cattle into the Bear Paw Mountain country near Havre in Northern Montana. He liked the country and decided to locate and build up a herd of his own.

He became a prominent citizen and at one time was Havre's constable. He also became a world champion rodeo rider and roper and was head of the Havre Rodeo Association. George rode a beautiful saddle horse named Tony. When the cowboy roped a calf at a rodeo or an exhibition, Tony was trained to back up and hold the rope taut until the calf was safely tied. Then Tony, as well as Long George, would turn toward the grandstand and bow to the applauding audience.

But, sad to relate, there were two sides to this personable cowboy's character and to his career. He was secretly involved with a gang of men who ran liquor across the nearby Canadian border. Like many others, Long George began building up his own herd "with a long rope," stealing unbranded calves, not only from his neighbors but from Canadians. It has been said that he actually stole back some of the calves which he had sold to nearby ranchers before the buyers had had time to brand them!

56

Long George was inordinately fond of horses and of fancy clothes. As one old cowboy of that day put it, "Long George was the best dressed cowboy on Milk River." He traded a stolen saddle horse and three legally owned ones to a Havre dealer, E. C. Carruth, for a fancy Alaskan beaver coat. The owner of the stolen horse, Phil Clack of Havre, came along one day and recognized his horse in Carruth's corral. Mr. Francis, dressed in his fine beaver coat, was promptly apprehended on a Havre street.

The cowboy thought that because of his standing in the community, and his popularity in the country, he would be cleared of the charges. But the jury convicted him and he left town before the sentence could be pronounced. Francis lived as a fugitive from justice for the next year with a $1,000 reward offered for his capture. He hid out in the Missouri badlands. But after a full year of evading the law, he decided to come into Havre and give himself up. He rode his horse into town, down the Main Street, and up to the Courthouse door.

Long George demanded a retrial, and in a courtroom packed with spectators, was sentenced to six to ten years in the State Penitentiary at Deer Lodge. Francis stood up and secured the Judge's permission to speak. "Judge, I've always been a man of my word, and I need a few days to go see my girl before I begin serving my sentence."

Possibly because the defendant had voluntarily given himself up, or maybe because it was almost Christmas time, the judge granted the tall cowboy's request.

The day before Christmas in 1920, Long George borrowed a truck, loaded it with Christmas gifts, apples and candy, and started out for the lonely little country schoolhouse north of Havre where his sweetheart taught.

A howling northern blizzard came up suddenly, covering the trail and landmarks. After battling the driving sleet and snow for many miles over trackless prairie, George lost his way and the truck skidded over a steep cut-bank onto the thick ice of the Milk River. He was pinned beneath the wreck but managed to release himself, only to find that his leg was broken.

When George failed to return at the appointed time, the Hill County sheriff started out with a posse to look for him. They tracked him to the wrecked truck and with the bits of evidence there reconstructed the story of his wreck, his struggle to free himself from the overturned vehicle, and the broken leg which made it impossible for him to walk to safety. A few burned matches and some charred seat cushions were mute testimony of the injured man's attempt— and failure—to build a fire and keep himself from freezing to death.

The posse picked up a faint trail in the snow and this led them to George's lifeless body about three miles from the truck. He had made a rude splint for his leg from an apple crate and had attempted to crawl to the school house. But when the sheriff's men found him, slashed throat and a pocketknife in the snow told the story of the final decision to die by his own hand rather than wait for slow and frigid death.

It is said that on the day of Long George's funeral his gallant horse, Tony, with an empty saddle followed the casket in the funeral procession to the cemetery. After one of the largest funerals ever held in Havre, the long, lean body of George Francis was laid to rest in the cemetery on a hill overlooking the town.

Legend has it that the "schoolmarm" sweetheart from the little country school near the Canadian border remained faithful to the memory of the Robin Hood cowboy who died trying to bring Christmas treats to her and her charges. She became a well known Montana educator, but never married.

---

The author of this poignant Montana winter story has lived a life deserving of book-length treatment. Her parents, Mr. and Mrs. Nathaniel McGriffin, came to Montana in 1880, establishing a ranch in North Central Montana. She married one of Montana's famed cowboys, Ambrose (Kid Amby) Cheney, in 1903, and they raised a family of seven sons and one daughter. Before Mr. Cheney's death in 1964, they celebrated their 50th and 60th wedding anniversaries. Mrs. Cheney, who now lives in Portland, Ore., is still remarkably busy, writing her lively and historically significant memories.

57

*(handwritten notes on image: "aptured in Colorado Dec. 1913" near left photo; "Jany 1914 Captured at Kamloops BC" near Cochran description)*

JESSE J. SCOBLE

1736

JESSE J. SCOBLE

# $150.00 Reward

## For Arrest and Detention Until an Officer Can Come and Get Them.

$100.00 will be paid for the arrest of Jesse J. Scoble, and $50.00 for the arrest of Calvin W. Cochran. Both men wanted in Blaine County, Idaho, for Cattle and Horse Stealing. They have been going under the name of Howard and passing as brothers.

## Descriptions:

### JESSE J. SCOBLE---

Name, Jesse J. Scoble, alias J. H. Howard. Age, 23 years; height, 5 feet 8¾ inches; weight, 165 pounds; complexion, medium; hair, dark brown, now bleached lighter; eyes, brown, wears nose glasses as a disguise; nose, prominent; occupation, laborer, good horse man; born and raised in Muldoon, Idaho. Marks and scars: Brown mole side right cheek; white spot near left nipple; brown mole on right side below right nipple; large irregular scar in palm of right hand, caused by burn; hand dwarfed; long scar at base of right palm near wrist; LEFT HANDED; scar on back of left elbow above joint; small wart on little finger right hand; long scar on top and side right thumb; long flat feet. September 15, 1913, he was seen wearing brown suit, tan shoes, black derby hat.

### CALVIN W. COCHRAN---

Alias Max Cochran, Alias Fred Howard.

Age, 23 years; height, 5 feet 8 1-3 inches; weight, 180 pounds; complexion, swarthy; hair, medium brown, straight, heavy; eyes, dark brown; occupation, laborer and rider, good with horses; American. Marks and scars: Scar on inside right forearm, below elbow; wart on inside second finger right hand; scar on tip of left thumb, underneath; second toe of right foot is shorter than others; long scar on front of right ankle; vaccination scar on left upper arm; TATTOO, 5 petal flower with circle in center, with stem below, BLUE INK, on inside of left lower arm; wart on back of second finger right hand; swarthy skin; last seen September 15th wearing dark suit, new tan shoes, black crusher hat; generally wears large white hat.

These men will be found around redlight districts, or livery barns. If located, arrest, hold and wire my expense.

# Aaron Clements,

## Sheriff of Blaine County, Idaho.

Dated Hailey, Idaho, September 26th, 1913.

NEWS-MINER LINOTYPE AND ELECTRIC PRINT, HAILEY, IDAHO.

# $250.00 REWARD

For the arrest and detention of Henry George, better known as "Baldy George." Height about 5 feet 8 in., weight about 140 lbs, eyes blue---sharp, complexion light---weather tanned, bald headed except fringe of light colored hair, rather broad square shoulders, has small feet, is restless, quick acting and speaking, good rider, cowboy and sheep herder. Usually wears slouch hat pulled down over eyes, is smooth talker with slight Southern accent, talkative when drunk, frequents saloons and sporting houses when in town, has some gold in teeth, rather wide forehead and prominent chin---medium. May have assumed name and allowed beard to grow. Indicted for horse stealing and broke jail on Sept. 25th, 1913, at Sturgis, South Dakota. $200. reward is offered by Meade County and $50. by Joseph Collins, Sheriff.

Wire.                    JOSEPH COLLINS,
                                          Sheriff,
                              Sturgis, So. Dak.

# Wanted for Horse Stealing

# $100
## REWARD

I am authorized to offer $100 reward for Cal Monroe and Clive Daugherty, who drove three head of horses from the Grand Ronde country into Wallowa county, Oregon, prior to March 17, 1915.

Monroe looks to be about 25 years old, about six feet tall, usually wears white hat with broad rolled brim and crown pushed up to a peak, rather bony face, smooth shaved, kindly odd eyes and look as though they were weak; very light complexion, and weighs about 175 lbs.

Daugherty is 21 years old, but looks like he was nearer 18, very small for his age, weighs about 135, has rather large nose with large end, height about five feet and three or four inches.

I hold warrant for both men. Arrest and wire at my expense.

## F. M. Halsey, Sheriff
### Asotin, Washington.

## $100 REWARD $100

For the arrest of Ira Kinder, alias Harve Hamilton, for horse stealing. When last seen he wore a brown suit of clothes and white hat. Description—About 5 feet, 10 or 11 inches; weight about 170 lbs; age about 27 years; light complexion; stutters a little when he talks, especially when excited; square shouldered but carries his head down when he walks; walks with a very quick step Brother officers get busy as we want this man badly.　　　Wire J. W. BLAIR, Sheriff,

Eads, Colorado.

*Aug. 20, 1912*

# STRAYED OR STOLEN

## $75.00 REWARD

One brown mare 12 years old, branded **7 H ┼** on left hip; wire cut on front of both hocks. One black mare 9 years old, unbranded; wire cut on one forearm, also wire cut on front of hind leg. Both mares have star in forehead and white hind feet; both heavy in foal. One black mare, weight 1250 pounds, 5 years old, white spot in forehead, branded **Ƶ** on left hip.

Owner will pay $50 for return of animals. I will pay $25 for apprehension of thief.

Wire information at my expense.

SILAS S. LAMB, Sheriff
Fort Morgan, Colo.

# WANTED
## For Horse Stealing
## $25.00 REWARD

A. T. Harrison, age 29 years, weight 150 lbs., height 5 5 5-8, stocky build, deep chestnut hair, slate colored eyes, dark complexion. Has oval scar below left elbow, scar on second joint left thumb, and another on right little finger. Nail on left middle finger deformed.

This man has served one term in Walla Walla penitentiary, committed from Spokane May 2, 1911 and father is now in penitentiary.

This reward will be paid for capture or information leading thereto. If located, immediately notify

## J. A. Level,
### Sheriff Lincoln County
## Davenport, Washington

# $25.00 REWARD

## FOR ARREST
## Wanted for Horse Stealing

NAME: Earnest Miller; about 35 years old; 6 feet 4 inches tall; weight, about 195 pounds, straight built; medium dark complexion; brown hair; gray eyes; smooth shaven; prominent jaws; sharp chin; sort of talks through nose, and does not have much to say; usually wears a high crown black hat, and carries a six shooter in shoulder scabbard.

Generally goes about the country horse back and does some ranch work in Idaho and Montana.

This man stole a horse out of the Centennial Valley of this county in October, 1912, and went to Idaho. He cashed a check at Dubois, Idaho, and was supposed to be headed for St. Anthony, Idaho.

Was again seen in Centennial about November 15th, riding a bay horse and was supposed to be headed down the Madison river and was going to Livingston, Mont.

Please keep a sharp lookout and if located, arrest, hold and wire at my expense.

### O. C. GOSMAN, Sheriff,
#### Dillon, Montana.

Dated December 2nd, 1912.

# REWARD!

# $50

STOLEN FROM BELGRADE, MONTANA, JULY 15, 1911,

## One Iron-Grey Mare

WEIGHT ABOUT 1,000 POUNDS· BRANDED [UP] ON THE LEFT
SHOULDER.  ALSO SADDLE, MADE IN GLENDIVE, AND A RAW-
HIDE ROPE.  WILL PAY THE ABOVE REWARD UPON THE CON-
VICTION OF PARTY WHO STOLE THE OUTFIT

WIRE ANY INFORMATION AT MY EXPENSE

## A. H. Sales, Sheriff

BOZEMAN, MONTANA.

Thompson Falls Mont.
Aug.30/13

Sheriffs Office
Missoula Mont..

There has been stolen  four head of work horses the last week

from the ranch of George Woodworth near Wisdom Mont.

Two of them are grey mares and two of them are black mares

weighing from 1200 to 1500 pounds each and are branded with

ED    on the left shoulder.

Arrest anybody found with these horses in their possession and

wire me at my expense, or wire D.V.Irwin Sheriff of Beaverhead Co.

William Moser
Sheriff of Sanders County

By *Fred Woodworth*
Deputy Sheriff

# $200 REWARD

The undersigned will pay the sum of $100.00 for the arrest of one

## Cliff Regan

alias Pat Russel, George Davis, C. W. Regan, Frank Moore, George Lister. Also will pay the sum of $100.00 for recovery of horse and saddle stolen by same party at Independence, Cal., on the night of July 19th, 1912.

**Description of Cliff Regan:** Age about 40 years, weight about 150 pounds, height about 5 feet 7 or 8 inches, rather thin lips, high cheek bones, gray eyes, avoids looking person in the eye, nose narrow at the top, rather wide and heavy at the bottom, scar at point of left elbow, scar center of breast, scar left cheek bone, scar front of head. Has shot wound on right heel and walks with a slight limp. Hair reddish cast, may be dyed, smooth shaven, florid complexion.

### Description of Horse and Saddle

Large bay saddle horse, tall, rangy and stylish appearance, weight from 1100 to 1200 pounds, single footer or pacer, white spot about the size of a dime in hollow above right eye, small white spot on left shoulder, slight wire cut on right fore leg between knee and breast, right hind foot white, age about nine years. Has light brand GL on right hip.

New saddle, just oiled, made by Keystone Bros., 15-inch tree, Visalia special bulge fork, 2 3-4 inch double stirrup leathers, 1 1-2 inch ladigo, galvanized iron bound stirrups, basket stamped, plain Spanish bit, slit ear head stall, reins nickle mounted, had long lasso rope with iron honda.

Am very desirous of getting back horse and outfit. Would like to have all peace officers look over the stock in all stables, feed corrals, etc., and interview all dealers, in order to obtain them if possible.

I desire to impress upon you the dangerous character of this man, and would suggest that you take no chances in making arrest, as he has declared that he would never surrender.

I hold warrant for arrest. Wire any information to

**CHAS. A. COLLINS, SHERIFF,**

Independence, Inyo County, Cal.

Sheriff C. P, Ferrell of Washoe county, Nevada, also offers a reward of $50.00 for the arrest of Cliff Regan, alias George Davis, etc.

Second Issue.

# $400.00 REWARD

Mr. Geo. E. Walker, of Arco, Blaine County, Idaho, will pay the following rewards for horses stolen from the range near his ranch on Lost River:

*$10.00 per head will be given for the return of the following horses, and also $250.00 FOR THE THIEF:*

BRANDS

| | |
|---|---|
| Black Mare, with sucking colt, | R G W |
| Gray Mare | " " |
| Bay Mare | " " |
| Brown Mare, with sucking colt | " |
| Buckskin Mare " " | " |
| Brown Horse | " |
| Bay Mare | " |
| Bay Mare 2 years old | " |
| Bay Mare 1 year old | " |
| Sorrel Horse 2 years old | " |
| Sorrel Horse 2 years old | " |
| Roan Horse 2 years old | " |
| Brown Horse 1 year old | " |
| Bay Mare 2 years old | " |

All of the above on Right Thigh.
White Mare branded M on Left Thigh.

These horses, with others stolen from this section of the state, will no doubt be driven across the country to the main line and shipped to eastern states.

The intention of the gang working is to split them up and take a bunch to the Twin Falls country, and the other bunch to Ontario, or near there.

They may change their minds and go to other shipping points.

They will peddle them to a horse buyer, if any in the country; if none in the country, they will ship them.

Kindly notify your deputies and the constables in your county to keep a close watch for shipments going out, and when a shipment is to be made, INSPECT THE BRANDS. Don't sit down and ask them what the brands are and give them a certificate without ever seeing the stuff.

I make this request for the reason that I railroaded for fifteen years, and many a car of horses and cattle I have billed out of these western states with a certificate of the brands attached to the billing signed by constables and deputy sheriffs when I knew for a positive fact that they had never been near the cattle or horses.

*Let's all get together and watch this business closer, and there will not be so much of it.*

*Wire any information at my expense.*

## Aaron Clements,
### Sheriff of Blaine County, Idaho.

HAILEY, IDAHO, SEPT. 20th, 1913.

NEWS-MINER LINOTYPE AND ELECTRIC PRINT, HAILEY, IDAHO.

Notknownhe.
Salem

*Aug. 14, 1914*

WANTED FOR HORSESTEALING
Chas· Cook, Alias Webster,
ex-convict of the Idaho
Penitentiary; Age 42 years;
Height, 5 feet 5½ inches;
medium complexion; light
brown hair; gray eyes; wt.
about 145 pounds.
Cook is a fiddler and also
a pugilist, sometimes boxes
a preliminary at prizefights.
When last seen was travelin
with team and wagon in company with a large woman and
three children, one a baby
with hairlip.
Address all information to
D. H. Kerfoot, Sheriff
Vale, Malheur County, Oregon.

# STOLEN

Dec. 10, 1911

One Gray Horse branded **20** on left stifle. Weight about 1400 pounds. Age about 12 years.

One Roan Horse branded **20** on left stifle. Weight about 1200 pounds. About 12 years old.

One Buckskin Horse branded **F S** on left shoulder. Weight about 1100 pounds. Black stripe down back with tiger legs. About 15 years old.

## Above are Work Horses.

One Black Mare branded **A C** on right shoulder with **J** on right stifle. Weight about 1200 pounds. About 10 years old.

One Blue Mare branded **J** on right stifle. Weight about 1200 About 10 years old.

## Arrest Parties Found with Same; Hold and Wire

### W. K. HUNTINGTON,
#### CHALLIS, IDAHO.

## Sheriff of Custer County, Idaho.

# $25.00 Reward!

## STOLEN

*From the pasture of Lane & Maunders on Little Wood River, in Muldoon, Blaine County, Idaho, about Sept. 30th, 1913*

*One bay horse, 4 years old, weight about 1150 or 1200 pounds, branded (Lazy J) on neck, right side under mane; wire scratches on back; mane and tail wore off some by rubbing. - - - - -*

This reward will be paid for return of horse, or for information leading to the arrest of the thief. Wire any information to

AARON CLEMENTS, Sheriff,

HAILEY, IDAHO.

News-Miner Print

# $50.00 REWARD!

Office of the Sheriff             North Yakima, Wash., July 13, 1914

*To Any Officer:*

A reward of $50.00 will be paid for the arrest and delivery to a Yakima County officer of a man named Charles Matney, charged with cattle stealing, who broke jail here July 5th, 1914. His description runs as follows: Age about 30 years, height about 5 feet 7 inches, weight 140 pounds; light brown hair, brown eyes, smooth shaven, medium complexion; has scars on his body which appear to be knife wounds. When last seen was wearing a pair of red tan button shoes, soft black hat, blue shirt, dark pants and coat, inclined to blue in color. Is a blacksmith by trade, and sometimes dresses like a cow-boy.

Please apprehend this man if he comes your way; hold, and wire this office at our expense.

J. METZGER,
Sheriff Yakima County, Wash.

# $200   REWARD   $200

**A reward of Two Hundred Dollars will be paid by me for the arrest and detention, until I can come with papers to claim him, for the following described man, who is wanted for stock stealing in Grant County, Oregon.**

Name, Monard Fix; about 40 years of age; height, about 5 feet, 10 inches; weight, about 150 or 160 pounds; has medium light brown hair; is of a fair complexion; is a rather thin featured sort of a fellow; has thin Roman nose; walks erect; has the habit of pulling hat down low over eyes or well back on head; when standing around talking, has habit of putting hands in front in pants belt; will likely be found handling stock; is horse trader; rides a good horse and has a good saddle; when last seen was in Umatilla county, Oregon, about April 15, this year.

**Arrest, hold and wire at my expense. Said reward holds good until December 1, 1913.**

**Dated at Canyon City, Grant County, Oregon, September 19, 1913.**

**WM. WELSH,**

**Sheriff of Grant County, Oregon.**

# WANTED FOR
# HORSE STEALING

# ERNEST WILLIAMS

Nativity, Idaho

Occupation, Laborer

Crime, Grand Larceny

Age, 24

Height, 5 feet, 8⅝ inches

Weight, 146 pounds

Complexion, Light

Teeth, Good, Regular

Color of Hair, Dark Blonde

Eyes, Gray

## BERTILLON MEASUREMENTS

| | | HEAD | | | |
|---|---|---|---|---|---|
| Height 1 m | 74.3 | Length | 19.4 | L. Foot | 25.5 |
| | | Width | 14.8 | L. Mid. F. | 11.1 |
| Outs 1 m | 78.0 | Cheek Width | 13.2 | L. Lit. F. | 8.4 |
| Trunk | 91.5 | R. Ear Length 7.0 | | L. Forearm | 45.7 |

Last seen at Arco, Idaho, near Hailey, January 8th, 1915, and supposed to be headed for Wyoming or Montana. He is a cowboy and ranch hand and will probably seek this kind of work. Is an ex-convict from the Nevada State Penitentiary and only recently released from that institution.

The above photograph is a good likeness of Williams, but when seen at Arco, was growing a moustache which no doubt he will continue in order to make identification more difficult.

If located, arrest, hold and wire at my expense and I will immediately send officer with proper papers.

Dated at Vale, Oregon, this 3rd day of September, 1915.

## BEN J. BROWN, Sheriff.

(Card No. 12, Second Issue.)

# $150.00 Reward!!

I hold warrants for the arrest of Frank and Ralph Jamison for the theft of two Buick automobiles. The description of the cars are as follows:

> One 7-passenger model D55, 1916, dark green body with black fenders, engine No. 192915, frame No. 192668 under left headlight. One 5-passenger model D45, 1916, green body with black fenders and hood, engine No. 204618 under left headlight.

These cars were stolen from the Inland Auto Company of Prineville, Oregon, May 15, 1916. It is believed they are still carrying our dealer's license No. 186, large red sign. The men are both tall and slender. Ralph is smooth shaven while Frank, who drove the large car, had a mustache when he left here. Both men are married and their wives are traveling with them. One of the couples had one child with them.

These cars passed through Norris, Montana, a short time ago, apparently traveling in an easterly direction.

The London-Lankshire Insurance Co., will pay $100.00 reward for recovery of big car and the Inland Auto Co., of Prineville, Oregon, will pay $50.00 for arrest of the men and recovery of the smaller car. If apprehended hold men and cars and wire collect.

E. B. KNOX
Sheriff of Crook County,
Prineville, Oregon

# $50. REWARD

Offered by the St. Paul Fire and Marine Ins. Co.
for recovery of

# Paige "36"
## Automobile

Five-passenger, touring, 1915 model; motor No. 16697, chasis No. 16708; license No. 37328; color: body dark blue, hood and fenders black; upholstering black, with brown detachable covering; Goodrich non-skid tires; Gray & Davis electric starting and lighting system; square nickel plated bumper in front. Car stolen in Spokane, August 29.

## PLEASE POST IN A CONSPICUOUS PLACE

Wire or telephone any information to M. C. Hunter & Co., Old National Bank Building, Spokane, Wash.

**WALTER A. FRAZIER,**
*Special Agent*

607 Paulsen Building, Spokane, Wash.

# Automobile Stolen

## 30 horse power Case Car

Gray color, 1913 model, Car No. 19,283, Engine No. 17,322, Wash. License No. 19,050. Nobby tire on right hind wheel, smooth tire on left hind wheel, swinging nobby on rear; lights out of order; Disco handle broken off.

Jacob Brandt of Oakesdale, Wash., offers a reward of $25.00 for information leading to the recovery of the above described car. Wire all information collect to

**WM. COLE,**

Sheriff of Whitman County,
Colfax, Washington.

September 22.

Send copy to Garages

# $50.00 REWARD!!

## $25.00 FOR RECOVERY

## 1913 OVERLAND ROADSTER

## $25.00 for Arrest and Conviction of Thief

STOLEN from in front of The Paulsen Building, Spokane, Washington, on the morning of May 1st, a 1913 Overland Roadster, Model 69, fully equipped.

License Number, Wn. 23395.

Factory Number, 17953.

Overland Model 69 R

NOTIFY

## UNION MARINE INSURANCE COMPANY

### OF LIVERPOOL

McCREA & MERRYWEATHER, Agents

Main 7121    A-1907

Sprague Ave. and Howard St.

Spokane, Washington

**Please Post in a Conspicuous Place**

SHAW & BORDEN CO. 140548

# $30.00 REWARD

# Automobile Stolen

A 1915 Ford Roadster, Engine No. 742100, Car No. 691452, Whitman county Temporary License No. 1266, lower wind shield broken and piece of glass gone, new back fenders with iron plates on top and beneath fenders as patches, three holes on top of car, left front fender bent. Two straight rods projecting out in front used to support bumpers, Claxton horn. Cut out and forked rod to reinforce the radius rod added to the car, grips, robes and coats in the back seat at the time it was taken.

The car belongs to Willis Mahoney, of Tekoa, Wash., and was taken from in front of the Opera House at that place on the night of July 2, 1915. Mr. Mahoney offers a reward of $30.00 for the recovery of the car.

Arrest any one found in possession of the car and wire me at my expense

## WM. COLE, Sheriff

COLFAX, WASH., July 9, 1915.

REVISED CIRCULAR NO. 2

# $155 REWARD
## for Automobiles Stolen

A 1915 Ford Roadster, Engine No. 742100, Car No. 691452, Whitman county Temporary License No. 1266, lower wind shield broken and piece of glass gone, new back fenders with iron plates on top and beneath fenders as patches, three holes on top of car, left front fender bent. Two straight rods projecting out in front to support bumpers, Claxton horn. Cut out and forked rod to reinforce the radius rod added to the car; grips, robes and coats in the back seat at the time it was taken.

The car belongs to Willis Mahoney, of Tekoa, Wash., and was taken from in front of the opera house at that place on the night of July 2, 1915. Mr. Mahoney offers a reward of $30.00 for the recovery of the car.

On the night of September 3rd A. C. Hemingway's automobile was stolen from his garage about four miles west of Thornton. The thief or thieves unlocked the padlock on the garage and pushed the car out into the road before starting it.

The car is a 1915 Five-passenger Ford, practically new, regularly equipped, electric lights; engine number, 694241; car number, 686729; Washington license number, 7225; slight scratch on top of left hind door. In the car was a dark coat and vest with letters addressed to A. C. Hemmingway, Thornton, Wash. The thief wore about a No. 8 new pair of pointed-toed shoes.

Mr. Hemmingway will give a reward of $50.00 for the recovery of the car and $50.00 for the arrest and conviction of the party or parties who took it.

Stolen from in front of the Chadwick Hardware Store on Main Street, in Colfax, between 2 and 5 p. m. on September 10th, five-passenger Ford car, 1913 model equipped with electric lights. Car No. 228917, engine No. 245387, Washington license No. 22632. Radiator dented slightly from jamming. **V SHAPED PATCH ON TOP COVER** on left side, new chain tread tires on rear wheels and smooth tires on front; pet cock underneath engine broken off and cord put in.

The above car belongs to Dr. Strain of this city, who offers $25.00 for its recovery.

Arrest any one found in possession of any of these cars and notify me at my expense. I will come with proper papers and bring them back.

As this is the season of the year cars come to the garages for repair I would urge all repair men to check up on cars that are brought to them. Please post this notice in a conspicuous place and see that each garage in your town has one.

2nd Edition Nov. 1915.

**WM. COLE, Sheriff.**
Colfax, Whitman County, Washington.

# WANTED FOR MURDER
## AND SAFE BLOWING

Willia̅ ̅ ̅ ̅ ̅ Dillon, Joseph Conroy

This ̅ ̅ ̅ ̅ ̅ of the trio that blew the safe
i̅ ̅ ̅ ̅ ̅ ̅ d the Night Watchman
̅ ̅ ̅ ̅ ̅ ̅ August 29, 1914.

DESCRIPT ̅ ̅ ̅ ̅ eight, 5 feet 10¾ inches; Hair, dark brown
Complexion, ̅ ̅ ̅ ̅ ̅ ̅ ue; Weight, 169 pounds.

TATO ̅ ̅ ̅ ̅ ̅ s on right fore arm.

̅ ̅ ̅ ̅ ̅ are shoulders, long features, sm̅

̅ ̅ ̅ ̅ tin 24915, Portland 165̅

FINGER PRINT
CLASSIFICATION

1   u   I
—————————  1̅
9   u   00

Murder, Arson, Rape, Manslaughter

# MURDER MOST FOUL

**W**hile murder itself, alas, needs no definition, perpetrators in this volume's time period faced methods of execution different than they would today: hanging and firing squad. In Nevada and Utah, the condemned had the right to choose. Nevada even offered a truly modern method with its "execution machine": three rifles aimed at the right spot and fired by an unseen controller. It was used in 1913 for the state's only execution by gunfire; Nevada's next execution, nine years later, was the nation's first in a gas chamber.

From the colonial period to the nineteenth century, arson (with no resulting deaths) and rape were capital crimes in most states.

*$1000 Reward*

# $400

## Reward For Arrest of

# FRED CLANCY

### Suspected of the Murder of Oscar Olson, Near Fernwood, Benewah County, Idaho.

## DESCRIPTION:

Height 6 ft. or 6 ft. 1 in.; weight 163 lbs.; age 37 to 40; light complexion; dark blue eyes; light brown hair; sometimes lets beard grow, which is lighter than his hair and of a reddish cast. Is very slim; has straight shoulders but stoops; has very long legs and long arms; big long and thin hands; wears number 9 shoe; 15½ shirt; has scar under left eye, on cheek bone, said scar is dark but not large.; has long face, with long chin, thin lips and thin nose. Teeth are even, but dirty. Chews snuff. Smokes cigarettes at times, and his fingers are much stained. He has a slight accent, might be of Scotch or English descent; talks rather slowly. Seems to have poor lungs, and complains of having the asthma very bad. Walks rather slow but regular. Was wearing black hat, cheap gray coat and gray pants, but pants did not match coat.

He left Spokane, Washington, on a Northern Pacific train for the West on the evening of December 6th 1915; was carrying a blue suit of clothes and a black overcoat which had just been cleaned, and which were the property of Oscar Olson.

I will pay the sum of Two Hundred Dollars to any party apprehending and delivering the said Fred Clancy to me.

The relatives of the said Oscar Olson also offer and will pay an additional reward of Two Hundred Dollars for the apprehension and delivery of said Fred Clancy.

Dated at St. Maries, Idaho, this 12th day of January, A. D., 1916.

### C. W. LEAF,

Sheriff of Benewah County,
State of Idaho.

# 1441

## $250.00 REWARD

## "One Fingered" GEORGE

Big, dark complexioned man, Brown Eyes, walks very erect. *(Rawlins Wyoming)* (OVER)

This man is wanted for murder, escaped from prison, is described as follows: 5 feet, 10¼ inches high, hair chestnut age 40, weighs about 185 to 200, dim vac scar above left elbow, all fingers off right hand but the index finger, pit of back and legs hairy; has a loud, hearty, peculiar, attractive laugh, is a good cow puncher, ropes and shoots left handed, does not drink or use tobacco, nor gamble, very attentive to the ladies, writes a very poor hand, has very little education; want this man very much, he also deserted a good wife and 6 children.

Wire all communications to

**FELIX ALSTON,**
Warden,

**Rawlins, Wyoming.**

(over)

JAN 21 1914    2003.26.194

# THE APPLE-PICKING KILLER

Fall settled like a heavy hand over the Day and Hansen Ranch on the upper Blackfoot River. There, in the quiet Montana countryside, two cowpokes tried their luck at a game of cards.

M. McMillan watched his stack of poker chips grow. Young Charles Hecker watched his disappear. It didn't take long for Hecker to run out of cash, and tempers flared.

Hecker's lousy turn of fortune hit a nerve. He stomped off for the nearest pub to drink his few remaining earnings. But the longer he sat, the madder he got. One thought lead to another, and he snatched up a box of ammo for his .32-caliber Colt. Drunk and armed he turned back for the ranch.

Ranch hand Sam Quale shared a tent with McMillan. In the dark of night, Quale woke to the ravings of a madman. Someone had entered their tent and was ordering McMillan to remove his pants. The same voice told Quale to lie still, keep his mouth shut, and he wouldn't get hurt.

McMillan removed his trousers as instructed. But while doing so he snuck closer to the gun-toting robber. Once in arm's reach he jumped on the man and wrestled him to the ground. It would prove to be a mistake.

Quale didn't stick around to see how the fight would turn out. He ran out the back of the tent.

Moments later two shots sounded in the dark. Cowboys rushed to the scene to find McMillan down, mortally wounded and lying in the dust. The hole in his heart proved to be fatal.

The next morning, news of the shooting reached Powell County Sheriff Joe Neville. The sheriff made the long trip to Helmville, accompanied by coroner Harry Peterson and attorney Albert Bien. They knew Hecker was their man. They also knew exactly where to find him.

"How well the officer reasoned is shown by the fact that on reaching Drummond, he soon found that the fugitive had been seen near that place," the *Silver State Post* reported.

The good people of Drummond had seen the fugitive plucking apples from a tree. They were eager to report the news. Neville caught up to the apple-picking killer at dusk and closed in for the arrest.

Hecker couldn't know that the farmhouse he took refuge in was actually owned by one of the deputies. So when lawmen appeared in the doorway looking ten feet tall if they were a foot, Hecker froze.

Officers hauled Hecker back to Deer Lodge for trial. Quale was the closest thing the prosecution had to a witness. He couldn't identify Hecker as the guilty man—it had been too dark that night in the tent—and Hecker was excused by a hung jury.

# THE WESTERN UNION TELEGRAPH COMPANY

INCORPORATED

## 25,000 OFFICES IN AMERICA.     CABLE SERVICE TO ALL THE WORLD

Form 1864

## RECEIVED AT

66.UN.K. 81,  1 extra.

Deer Lodge Mont sept 12-11.

Sheriff Missoula.

Chas Hocker Aged 21 years smooth face,medium dark complexion slim
build slim face height 5,ft 9 inches weight about 150 pounds wore
a soft shirt blue coat blue overalls cut off at  shoe tops wore
 high brown shoes carried a 32 automatic colts revolver wanted by
sheriff of Powell county for the murder of M.McMillan,killed near
Helmville Mont sept 12th 1911,wire sheriffs office at Deer Lodge
Mont.

                              J.E.Neville

                                   Sheriff.

310-pm

57

# COLD-BLOODED KILLERS

Just about the time H. W. Herrick and his brother Orson were ready to close up shop and call it a night, two men entered their store. It wouldn't take these leading citizens of Lake County, California, long to realize their two customers were up to no good.

Instead of bearing smiles, the two bandits brandished a different sort of greeting. One quickly turned his gun on Orson and ordered him to stand still, to put his hands in the air, and keep his mouth shut.

Orson complied without hesitation. But Herrick had a different plan. Instead of putting his hands in the air, he attempted to wrestle the gun away from the second crook. His plan failed miserably and the bandit shot him dead. Herrick fell like a sack of marbles in front of the door.

With his brother murdered, Orson attempted no resistance as the crooks proceeded to ransack the store. His cooperation may have saved his life. Instead of killing Orson, the crooks bound and gagged him, then took whatever money he had on his person. He wouldn't be causing any trouble now as he could only watch the twin bandits pick the pockets of his dead brother.

There wasn't time to rob the safe. The crooks had to make their break and make it fast. A third bandit waited outside—his identity concealed by a mask.

With the three crooks together, and the robbery going terribly wrong, the trio mounted their steeds and made a desperate dash for the hills, completing what newspapers would call a "true Wild West–style killing."

The one who appeared to be the leader of the band rushed a dark horse into the night. His two accomplices followed in short order. Meanwhile, poor Orson finally broke his bonds, wasting no time in spreading the alarm.

Men across the city joined the chase, hunting for the killers of Orson's brother. It wouldn't take long for the law to catch up. By week's end police would have Edward Fitzgerald in custody.

All the officers had to do was wait at Fitzgerald's girlfriend's cabin up Bucksnort Canyon. Sure enough the villain showed up. He was soon arraigned on a charge of murder while his two accomplices remained at large.

"After a fruitless chase through three counties the posses engaged in the manhunt returned home on Monday on receiving word that the two bandits were positively seen in Napa eating a meal," reported the *Lake County Bee*. "The bandits visited Napa last Saturday and forced Mrs. Hardester to give them food."

While the two bandits remained at large in San Francisco, police assumed, Fitzgerald made his first court appearance.

"He protests his innocence and says he was the victim of a mistake," wrote the editor of the *Bee*. "In fair play to the prisoner, and to the county, any of his other remarks should not be published."

# $250 REWARD

## Wells Fargo & Company

offers (in lieu of any standing reward) a special reward of Two Hundred and Fifty Dollars ($250.00) for the arrest and conviction of bandit who on the night of May 6th, 1914, murdered H. W. Herrick, Agent for Wells Fargo & Company at Middletown, Lake county, California.

Felony warrant has been issued for Edward Fitzgerald, for robbery and murder.

Distribute this circular to Sheriffs and other officers. Search jails and State prisons.

EDWARD FITZGERALD,
alias Jack Moffitt.
This photo taken in prison.

EDWARD FITZGERALD,
alias Jack Moffitt.
This photo taken Aug. 15, 1914.

Height 5 ft. 8 in.; weight 150 lbs.; age twenty-five; complexion medium; eyes blue; hair black. Seven pit marks right cheek near eye. Indistinct tattoo marks on forearms. One upper front tooth out.

BERTILLON: 1.71.6 ** 19.1 ** 26.
1.81. ** 15.1 ** 12.5  46.8
.94.4 ** 6.7 ** 9.6

FINGER PRINT CLASSIFICATION: 1 U 0I 13
17 U 00

Telegraph all information to J. F. Seymour or C. Cain, Special Agents, Wells Fargo & Company, San Francisco; or L. O. McKelley, Sheriff, Lakeport, Lake county, California.

C. R. GRAHAM,
General Superintendent,
Wells Fargo & Company.

San Francisco,

May 20, 1915.

This cancels and supersedes reward circular of May 18, 1914, regarding Edward Fitzgerald and Robert Bell.

| CLASS OF SERVICE | SYMBOL |
|---|---|
| Day Message | |
| Day Letter | Blue |
| Night Message | Nite |
| Night Letter | N L |

If none of these three symbols appears after the check (number of words) this is a day message. Otherwise its character is indicated by the symbol appearing after the check.

# WESTERN UNION
# TELEGRAM

NEWCOMB CARLTON, PRESIDENT          GEORGE W. E. ATKINS, FIRST VICE-PRESIDENT

Form 1204

| CLASS OF SERVICE | SYMBOL |
|---|---|
| Day Message | |
| Day Letter | Blue |
| Night Message | Nite |
| Night Letter | N L |

If none of these three symbols appears after the check (number of words) this is a day message. Otherwise its character is indicated by the symbol appearing after the check.

### RECEIVED AT

74UNEK   50 BLUE   1 EX

        IRON MOUNTAIN MONT 1245PM OCT 2 1917

    SHERIFF GREENE

        MISSOULA MONT

WATCH TRAINS AND ASSIST ME  IN CAPTURE OF ALEX KUUM

COMMITTED MURDER AT SILDIX MONT  LAST NIGHT AGE TWENTY SIX

FIVE FOOT SIX INCHES LIGHT  HAIR LIGHT COMPLEXION CROOKED NOSE

WORE OLD GRAY SUIT CHOCOLATE  COLORED FEDERA HAT WALKS SHORT

AND QUICK LIVES IN BUTTE  WEIGHT ONE HUNDRED FORTY

                      CHARLES HOFFMAN SHERIFF

                                  328PM

*Captured @ Taft Mont*
*Oct. 3rd/17*

# $250.00 REWARD

I will pay Two Hundred and Fifty Dollars ($250.00) Reward for the arrest, detention and delivery to me, or my authorized representative of

## GEORGE FRANK PARSONS

for whose arrest I hold a warrant, and who is charged with the offence of arson committed at Lufkin, Angelina County, Texas, on the night of Sunday, March 2, 1913.

Said George Frank Parsons, whose photographs appear above was 26 years old in June 1912, but looks to be about 22 years old; he is about five feet ten inches in height, is round shouldered, stoops a little in walking and looks down. He has large blue eyes, light hair which is rather thin, high cheek bones, a large mouth and rather thick lips. He wears about number eight or nine shoe, talks very little, is distant in his manner and rather hard to get acquainted with; writes a smooth, plain scribbling sort of hand, is slow of motion and speech; does not chew, drink, curse or gamble, and smokes very little. On the night of March 2nd, 1913, when last seen, he had on a rather neat gray suit of clothes, and wore a medium wide brim black fuzzy hat. He also had and may wear a blue suit. He is slim in appearance and weighs about 140 or 150 pounds, perhaps as much as 160 pounds; is rather fair and Irish looking, wore open-face silver watch.

This man was, and for some three years had been employed by the Houston, East & West Texas Railway Co. at Lufkin, as warehouse clerk.

At the time of his disappearance, a printed coupon ticket, Form E-1000, No. 544, also disappeared. Said ticket has now been taken up, used, and has punched destination as Sacramento, Cal., was used on Westbound G. H. & S. A. train No. 9, leaving Houston, Texas, at 12:05 a. m. of March 4th, and leaving El Paso on S. P. train No. 9, on the morning of March 5th. Said ticket was taken up and exchange check given on said train. The exchange check has not yet appeared in collections of the S. P. Co., from which it appears that party left train short of final destination.

If this man is located, he should be arrested as a fugitive from justice and prompt notice given to the undersigned, or to M. C. Kahn, Special Agent, Houston, East & West Texas Ry. Co., Houston, Texas.

## R. V. WATTS
### Sheriff, Angelina County, Lufkin, Texas

# $500 REWARD

## Wanted for Murder

A reward of five hundred dollars is offered by the Governor of the State of Utah for information that will lead to the arrest and conviction of the person or persons who murdered J. H. Morrison and his son, J. Arling Morrison, in an attempted hold-up in this city on the night of January 10th, 1914.

### OTTO APPLEQUIST

The above is a good picture of one of the supposed murderers. Height, 5 feet 11 inches; weight, 175 pounds; age, 26; complexion, light; hair, light and quite thick; eyes, blue. Scar in center of forehead just above eyebrows. Regular features, and walks very erect. Will doubtless have large 38 automatic gun in his possession.

Reported to have the following tattoo marks: Right forearm, naked woman; left upper arm, Swedish emblem, also Swedish flag; the low emblem on forearm, sailor boy.

On December 31st, Otto Applequist was initiated as a member of the local branch of the Structural Ironworkers of Salt Lake, and may be carrying card of that Union. It is understood that he has a mother living in Chicago.

If arrested, wire me at my expense and I will send an officer with the necessary papers.

# MURDER FOR REVENGE

It was a cold January night when young Merlin Morrison stood at the back of the Salt Lake City store and watched the two gunman level their pistols at his father, simply to exact revenge on the family for a failed robbery years earlier.

But if this was revenge it went too far. When the gunsmoke cleared, Merlin's father, John H. Morrison, and his seventeen-year-old brother, John Jr., lay dead in a pool of blood.

The boy's story painted a disturbing picture. He told detectives how the two men rushed the store with their weapons drawn, their faces covered with handkerchiefs. The crooks made no effort to rob the register but instead turned their weapons on the defenseless John Morrison as he leaned over a sack of potatoes.

"We've got you now," one of the men said as he blasted a single shot at the elder Morrison. The bullet hit the man in the side of the chest; he fell with no time to stand in his own defense.

At the sound of gunfire, John Jr. took up the family pistol and charged into the store. Firing a single shot he hit one of the bandits before they replied in kind with several shots of their own. They hit the kid three times, killing him instantly.

After the smoke cleared and the crooks fled— one of them bleeding from the chest—young Merlin sounded the alarm. The citizens of Salt Lake City converged on the store.

Detectives sent an all-points bulletin to stations across the region. Officers then spread their dragnet far and wide. More than forty officers searched into the night. When the shift changed, many officers put on street clothes and stood at the train stations, keeping a lookout for the slayers.

In the early morning darkness, police finally caught a break, arresting W. J. Williams—a man they had found loitering on the corner near the grocery store.

Williams said he worked as a restaurant helper at the Salvation Army and was out for a midnight walk before going to bed. But police were suspicious—and they were right. They found blood on the man's handkerchief. They also learned that no one at the Salvation Army had ever heard of "Williams."

Utah Governor William Spry chose to post a reward for the arrest of the two killers. The governor issued a proclamation, insisting that his city would not be turned into a breeding ground for armed robbers.

The governor's proclamation worked. Nearly a week after the killing, two doctors told police they had treated a man for a bullet wound. The ball, fired by dead John Jr., had entered the man's side, pierced his left lung, and emerged through his back. The man had lost a good deal of blood, the doctors said, and was in a failing state.

According to the doctors, the man's name was Joseph Hill and he was resting at a friend's house where he'd been hiding for several days. Convinced that this was their man, police converged on the tidy home. While Hill made a move for his gun, police had him covered and the injured holdup was arrested without incident.

Hill was locked in the slammer despite the severity of his wound. Williams was also in custody, as was a man named Robert Erickson. As the days went on, police suspected that four men were involved in the shooting, the last being Otto Applequist, who was still at large.

# $500 REWARD

## BAY GORDON

TWO HUNDRED DOLLARS will be paid for the capture and delivery, or information that will lead to the arrest and detention of **BAY GORDON**, and THREE HUNDRED DOLLARS upon conviction of either forgery, or the murder of Peter A. Dieter near Rye, Colorado.

## DESCRIPTION:

Age 23, height 6 feet, weight 150 to 160 pounds.

Slender built, eyes blue gray, hair brown, smooth shaven.

Remarks: Good cowpuncher and rider, has been with the Dr. Carver show, is quiet of disposition, home at Bartlesville, Oklahoma.

**ARREST AND WIRE**

**F. E. McMILLAN, Sheriff
Pueblo, Colo.**

# $500 REWARD
## FOR
# MURDER

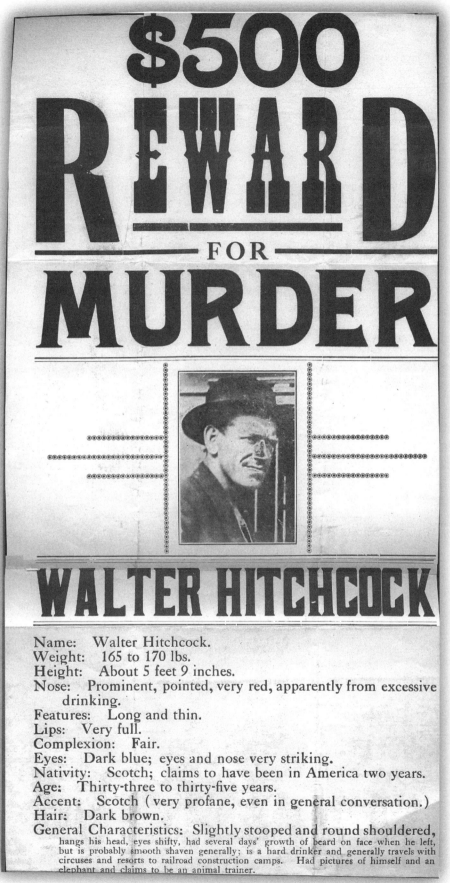

# WALTER HITCHCOCK

**Name:** Walter Hitchcock.

**Weight:** 165 to 170 lbs.

**Height:** About 5 feet 9 inches.

**Nose:** Prominent, pointed, very red, apparently from excessive drinking.

**Features:** Long and thin.

**Lips:** Very full.

**Complexion:** Fair.

**Eyes:** Dark blue; eyes and nose very striking.

**Nativity:** Scotch; claims to have been in America two years.

**Age:** Thirty-three to thirty-five years.

**Accent:** Scotch (very profane, even in general conversation.)

**Hair:** Dark brown.

**General Characteristics:** Slightly stooped and round shouldered, hangs his head, eyes shifty, had several days' growth of beard on face when he left, but is probably smooth shaven generally; is a hard drinker and generally travels with circuses and resorts to railroad construction camps. Had pictures of himself and an elephant and claims to be an animal trainer.

# $50.00 - REWARD - $50.00
# WANTED FOR MURDER
## BENINO FUERTE, a Mexican

Description:   Age about 35 or 40 years; weight about 175 or 180 lbs.; 6 feet tall; medium slender build; thin face with sallow or yellowish complexion.

When last seen, wore a small black mustache.   May now be smooth shaven.   Scar on neck.   Three fingers of right hand stiff.   Wore rather large, light soft hat, crown pointed at top. Bad actor.   Gun fighter.   Watch your jails.   Will hang around Indians and Mexicans.   Has been a wood chopping contractor.

This man shot and killed one Cardova, on Dry Creek, near Healdsburg, on the night of February 28, 1915.

My theory is that he went to Mexico after the killing, and is about due to return to the United States.

Arrest and wire any and all information to

J. K. SMITH, Sheriff,
Sonoma County, Calif.

Santa Rosa, Calif., May 6, 1918.

# THE KILLER WITH POOR MANNERS

The two lumberjacks spent the afternoon indulging in food and drink at a cabin in the woods near Santa Rosa, California. But when Benino Fuerte put his hat on inside the cabin, Frank Cardova decided to give the man a lesson in manners.

By all accounts, Fuerte wasn't pleased by the sudden education. In a fit of anger he left the table, called for his wife, and set off for the family tent. But he forgot his trunk, which sat in Cardova's cabin.

Fuerte stood over that trunk trying to figure out what to do with the .41-caliber revolver he now held in his hand. Cardova didn't appreciate the sight of the gun, or the lousy-mannered man who held it. He ordered Fuerte to put the pistol away, but Fuerte refused, storming into the yard with his trunk—the pistol perched on top.

Cardova had struck a nerve with the temperamental Fuerte. No sooner had Fuerte reached the yard did he stop, set down his trunk, and turn for the door. Cardova followed and the two men stood in the yard, eye to eye, separated only by their growing anger. Cardova said something. Fuerte retorted. Back and forth the words flew, followed by the single blast of Fuerte's pistol.

The lead ripped into Cardova's chest, punching its way between his shoulder blades. Paralyzed by the sudden and fatal blast, Cardova, who had been dining moments earlier, fell forward on his face, his arms pinned underneath the weight of his body.

But one shot wasn't good enough. Fuerte fired again, causing Cardova's limp body to jump. Deed done, the six-foot-tall cowboy with yellow skin and a black mustache disappeared into the vast California landscape.

Detectives reasoned that the villain was making his way to the hills of Napa County. There, they believed, he would work his way back to the Sierra Mountains where he once lived with his wife. But it would take more than three years for the Sonoma County sheriff to issue a wanted poster for Fuerte's arrest.

"My theory is that he went to Mexico after the killing and is about due to return to the United States," Sheriff J. K. Smith said.

"Watch your jails," the sheriff added. "He's likely to hang around Mexicans and Indians."

# Wanted for Rape

## $50 REWARD

**GEORGE HOEY:** About 5 feet 8; weight about 180 pounds; age 45 to 48, but don't look that old; very heavy head of light hair; light mustache; light complexion; blue eyes. Think he has some gold upper front teeth; very jolly and pleasant all the time; very talkative; generally dresses well, and was always known to wear a derby hat. Wanted badly.

If located, arrest and wire me at my expense. I hold warrant.

## ELIJAH ADAMS,

Sheriff of Madison County,
Virginia City, Montana.

PRESS OF MADISONIAN TIMES

# CIRCULAR

Rawlins, Wyo., October 4th, 1913

$ ~~25.00~~          # REWARD          $ ~~25.00~~

## Will be paid for the arrest and detention of

From this Prison, on the      day of      191

| | | | |
|---|---|---|---|
| Name | George Beckwith | Height, | 5 feet, 5¾ inches |
| Alias | | Color of Eyes | Slate Grey |
| County sent from | Sweetwater | Complexion | Medium |
| Crime | Manslaughter | Color of Hair | Light Chestnut |
| Term | 12 to 15 years | Age (about) | 24 Years |
| Nativity (nationality) | American | Weight (about) | 131# |
| Occupation | Baker | Build | Good |

## MARKS AND SCARS

Small cut scar at base of left index finger. Long cut scar extending from base of right third finger to above second joint. Curved scar on lower lip.

Peculiar actions and voice. Subject to fits.

REMARKS:

If arrested notify me by telegraph at my expense.

## FELIX ALSTON,
Warden.

# ROTTING BODY LAUNCHES MANHUNT ☞

When the two boys threw open the doors to the cabin at Canyon Lake that cool April morning they were in for the shock of a lifetime.

Stretched upon on the bed lay the body of twenty-two-year-old Luther Mullenix. The young gentleman from Three Rivers, California, had gone missing without a trace, leaving his friends and family baffled over his whereabouts.

Overcome by the scent of the man's decomposing body, Harrison Maxon and Fred Griffin dashed for the fresh air. The pair unwittingly found themselves at the heart of a growing mystery. Everyone had wondered where Mullenix had gone. Now the two boys knew the answer and were eager to break the news.

Fending off nausea, Maxon and Griffin ran for the nearest phone to spread the word. They dialed neighbor Mr. Griffith, who rushed to the scene. It didn't take Griffith long to reason that the boys were right—Mullenix was as dead as they come.

Griffith observed the pool of blood on the floor. He found the broken lamp, too, suggesting that a struggle had taken place. Struggle suggested murder. A gun was also found in the room, and the mystery grew.

Griffith didn't disturb the body to see if Mullenix had been shot. Instead, he left the scene as he found it, venturing off to call the Mt. Whitney Power House at nearby Hammond. News quickly spread and two cars raced to the scene, one containing the sheriff, the court reporter, and the photographer, the other hauling the deputy district attorney and coroner.

Answers were few and far between. Mullenix had left Three Rivers with a saddle animal and a packhorse for the Lake Canyon cabin. Days passed and nothing was heard of him. Friends tried to reach him over the government phone line but he never picked up.

Rumors were all that remained. Some said that when Mullenix left for the cabin he had carried a considerable quantity of liquor. What's more, a man later identified as Bert Shaffer allegedly was rooming at the cabin. Shaffer was also seen in Three Rivers riding Mullenix's horse. He was thought to have turned the animal loose, leaving the saddle in a deserted blacksmith shop. Then he vanished.

"This would seem to provide a motive for the murder, if murder it be," the *Visalia Daily Chronicle* read. "Some think that possibly the liquor had furnished material for a quarrel between the men, eventually leading to a fight and the killing."

The crime would be a tough one to crack. But California Governor Hiram Johnson signed on, issuing a $250 reward for the arrest and conviction of Shaffer.

# REWARD!

**EXECUTIVE DEPARTMENT,**
State of California.

WHEREAS, LUTHER MULLENIX, was on Feb. 19, 1916, murdered near Three Rivers, in Tulare Co., California, by BERT SHAFFER; and

WHEREAS, the said BERT SHAFFER is still at large, although diligent effort has been made to apprehend him.

NOW, THEREFORE, I, HIRAM W. JOHNSON, as Governor of the State of California, do hereby offer a reward of Two Hundred and Fifty Dollars.

# $250.00

for arrest and conviction of said BERT SHAFFER upon said charge.

IN WITNESS WHEREOF, I have hereunto set my hand and caused the Great Seal of the State of Calif. to be affixed this 5th day of April, 1916.

[ SEAL ]

**HIRAM W. JOHNSON,**
Governor.

Attest: FRANK C. JORDAN,
Secretary of State.

By FRANK H. CORY, Deputy

### DESCRIPTION OF BERT SHAFFER:

Age, about forty years; height, five feet nine or ten inches; weight, about one hundred and sixty pounds; complexion, medium (inclined to be dark); hair, dark brown, slightly streaked with gray, dark mustache.

MARKS AND PECULIARITIES: The eyeball of his right eye moves and twiches constantly when he is talking. The name "B. Slater" is tattooed on one of his arms. The second finger on one of his hands is stiff.

HABITS: He is a wandering laborer, drinks heavily and is likely to be arrested for drunkenness. He frequents saloons whenever he has money. When sober he is a very industrious worker at all kinds of ordinary labor.

He was last seen at Exeter, Tulare County, California, on the morning of February, 21, 1916 At that time he took a train for the South He wore a brown coat, gray trousers and a pair of new tan work shoes, Number 8.

PICTURE TAKEN NOVEMBER 20, 1912

# $250
# REWARD

## $250 REWARD FOR THE ARREST OF
# FRANK L. SMITH

Who confessed to murdering an officer, who was looking after freight car thieves for the Denver Northwestern Railway. Smith worked with another man named William Patrick Code, who :onvicted and is now serving a life term.

### NOVEMBER 20, 1912, THE DESCRIPTION OF SMITH WAS AS FOLLOWS:

BERTILLON—Height 79.0, Outer Arms 84.0, Trunk 94.5, Head Length 19.0, Head Width 14.2, Cheek 13 ength R. Ear 6.4, L. Foot 27.1, L. Mid. Fin. 11.9, L. L. F. 9.4, L. Fore A. 48.4.

Age 25, Height 5 ft. 10¾ in., Weight 160, Build medium, Hair Black, Dark Grey Eyes, Dark Complexio Occupation R. R. man, Born in Kentucky.

REMARKS—3rd finger off at 1st joint. Faint cut scar obl. 14.5 above wrist on inner side. Faint cut sc. 2.5 above knuckle on index finger on back of hand. 2 large cut scars on right side of stomach above groin cause y operation for appendicitis.

### HISTORY.

Smith was caught in Altus. Okla., and brought back to Brighton, Adams Co., Colo. On the night of Nov. 27 1912, he sawed the bars and escaped from jail. Smith was working as a car repairer and inspector and was caugl eaking open and robbing freight cars. He was well known in Oklahoma, where he was a railway car inspector an pairer. The County Commissioners of Adams County have just renewed their former offer of $250.00 reward fo any information that will lead to his arrest any where in the U. S., or any foreign country, if held until an office rives. Wire information, at our expense, to

## Leonard DeLue's Detective Agency

144 GAS BUILDING                                                        DENVER, COLO.

OR

### GEORGE E. RUCKER, Sheriff Adams County
BRIGHTON, COLORADO

# A DARK NIGHT AT UTAH JUNCTION

At midnight Frank L. Smith and William Patrick Code broke into the boxcar, looking for a nice suit and vest with pants to match.

They had done this a dozen times before and as Smith searched, young Code stood guard, peering up and down the rail yard for any hint of trouble.

Trouble was on its way in the form of watchman Mr. Stingley, a friendly man who knew the yard like the back of his hand. So when Code saw Stingley approach, he rapped on the car to warn Smith to stand still. He then asked Stingley for a match.

Stingley gave the man his match and passed down the yard. But his suspicions were roused and he circled back for a second look. When Stingley turned through the weed patch, Code leveled his pistol and fired.

"For God's sake," Stingley stammered. "What have you done, boys?"

"Shoot him again!" Smith screamed, jumping from the boxcar. Code pulled the trigger a second time and watched Stingley fall.

"I think I got him that time," Code said.

Standing over the dying watchman, Smith picked up a heavy bar and grinned the grin of an evil man. He raised the heavy bar and struck with all his might. He swung the iron six more times until he mangled Stingley's head.

Smith and Code were as bold as they were cruel. They continued working at the site for nearly a week and even joined their coworkers in demanding that the company place guards at the spot where Stingley had been murdered.

No one suspected them in the killing, they were sure. So after their job ended they went their separate ways and agreed to write. Code began loitering in the city, rooming at a downtown boarding house. Smith pawned the watchman's gun for $7 and left for Oklahoma with his pregnant wife.

But like a frat boy unable keep his mouth shut, Smith couldn't keep from telling of his conquests. In a drunken stupor he told a friend how he and Code had killed the watchman. Someone overheard the confession and told police, collecting the $250 reward.

Police had their men. Like seasoned pros, Smith and Code enamored the press with stories of girls, guns, and thefts. The press played a game of its own and turned the lies back on the suspects.

"The story that my wife was tired of me and tipped off the murder so she could get the reward and marry another man is an insult that I'd resent if I were out of here," Smith told one reporter.

On the night of November 27, Smith and fellow inmate James Stanton, a horse thief, hatched a plan. Using a saw smuggled into the jail by Stanton's wife, the duo sawed through the bars and escaped.

"He was cunning enough to get out, but I don't

think he is cunning enough to stay out," Code said when he learned of Smith's escape.

Smith, a desperate convict, was surrounded in Denver, dodging the law from alley to alley. But it was revealed that Smith had the skills of a ghost. He slipped past detectives on a midnight train and foiled all attempts to hunt him down.

Deputies suspected this cornered lion was looking for a fight. Police knew Smith wouldn't hesitate in taking another life, as he had little to lose.

But while the law hunted Smith, Stingley's widowed wife couldn't take any more. She grew weak, slipping into confusion and delirium. Within days paralysis set in. Her hands and arms failed her and she lay in her bed unable to move.

Six weeks after she lost her husband, the grief-stricken widow was dead. Doctors said she died of a broken heart. Her crushed spirit was too weak to fend off the reaper's shadow.

"Bereft of the man she loved, crushed by the weight of the tragedy on her heart, with reason gone, mind numb and spirit crucified, the little widow went broken and silent into death," reported the paper.

# WANTED FOR MURDER

## MANU PERI

A Finlander. Age, 23 years; Height, 5 feet, 7 inches; Weight, 155 pounds; Hair, medium light; Eyes, blue. Smooth, round face. Rather good looking. Wore brown suit of clothes and gray cap. Speaks very little English.

Wanted for the murder of Jacob Mlkkila, night of January 22nd, 1914

## ARREST AND WIRE AT MY EXPENSE.

## TIM DRISCOLL, Sheriff

**Silver Bow County**        **Butte, Montana**

# THE AXE KILLER

Agnes Loveless finally got a break from motherhood and returned home, reeling from the delights of a late-night dance in Dubois, Idaho.

But her married lover and occasional roommate wasn't pleased by the hour of her return. Walter Cairns, a jealous man, went at her with a volley of questions. Where had she been? Why was she so late? Then he went at her with an axe.

Cairn's tattoos flexed as he raised the axe and swung, sinking the blade down the middle of the woman's head. The forty-year-old maniac with gray hair and no eyebrows then left his mistress to die a slow death on the floor.

It was still dark when the woman's nine-year-old son stumbled across the gruesome scene.

"Her blood covered the floor and part of her brains were strewn about the room," the *Teton Peak Chronicle* reported.

Loveless was rushed to the hospital but there was little hope. Police turned her three children over to their grandparents as detectives took charge of the bloody scene.

Investigators learned that Loveless had taken up residence with Cairns. They also learned that Cairns went by the alias Will Smith, and Will Smith had a dark side.

Police were eager for a quick arrest. Sheriff John Fisher suspected that Cairns had fled shortly after assaulting the woman with the axe. They also knew where to find him. They caught the suspect the next night and hauled him back to the county jail.

Loveless soon died. Her children were orphaned. Cairns faced a charge of murder. It wasn't his first. He had broken jail several months earlier at Pocatello, accused of killing a man in Pebble, Idaho. Only days after his arrest for Loveless' murder, Cairns again escaped incarceration by sawing through the bars of his cell.

# WANTED FOR

# MURDER!

Walt Cairns, age about 40 years, height about 5 ft. 8 or 9 in., weight about 165 pounds, dark brown hair, slightly gray around ears, eyes bluish brown, medium complexion, has little or no eyebrows, small scar over right eye, tattoo of star on right hand between thumb and index finger, also tattoo of anchor same place on left hand; he wore a light colored hat, brown coat, red sweater, blue over-alls over black trousers

Walt Cairns is supposed to have murdered Mrs. Agnes Loveless, with an axe, at Dubois, Idaho, night of May 5th, 1916. He was arrested and taken to St. Anthony, Idaho, where he sawed out of the county jail on the evening of May, 18th, 1916

### Arrest, hold and wire all information at my expense

# JOHN T. FISHER, Sheriff
#### St. Anthony, Idaho

# WANTED—$2,000 REWARD!

*Shot & Killed @ Arcadia Cal Nov 19th/18. Killed Depy Van Vliet*

**DALE JONES**

**MARGIE JONES**

*Shot & Killed by Deputies @ Arcadia Cal. Nov*

## MURDER and TRAIN ROBBERY

DALE JONES is wanted in connection with the hold-up and robbery of Kansas City & Denison R.P.O. (Missouri, Kansas & Texas Railway) Train No. 27, at Koch Siding, near Paola, Kansas, July 10, 1918. All other members of the gang committing this train robbery are either dead or in custody.

At Colorado Springs, Colorado, September 13, 1918, Dale Jones shot and instantly killed Chief of Detectives John W. Rowan, and wounded other officers while resisting arrest on the train robbery charge. He had entered the city in a Marmon automobile, accompanied by his wife, Margie Jones, and Roscoe Lancaster, alias "Kansas City Blackie." All three participated in the battle with the officers, and Margie Jones drove the automobile while making their escape. Roscoe Lancaster was subsequently killed while resisting arrest at Kansas City, Missouri.

DESCRIPTION :—DALE JONES, alias Ford Engles, alias Charles Forbes, alias Denver Dean, alias Lloyd Dean, alias Howard Layton, alias Felix Kingman. Age 21; height 5 feet 10 inches; weight 135 pounds; light chestnut hair, worn very long in front; light complexion—now pale and rather thin; middle finger on right hand amputated below second joint; dresses well, good mixer and pleasant manners. Speaks English and Spanish.

He is an expert chauffeur and automobile mechanic, and usually drives stolen automobiles of either Buick, Cadillac, Hudson or Marmon make. It is believed that he frequently disguises himself in women's clothing, at many times wearing a woman's hat and coat when driving automobiles. He is always heavily armed and is a very desperate character.

MARGIE JONES, nee Margie Celano, alias Jewell Dillon, alias Jewell Celano, alias Margie Dean, alias Margie Layton. Italian, age 20; height 5 feet 1 5-8 inches; weight 100 pounds; slender; olive complexion; black hair; brown eyes; ears pierced; speaks Italian, English and Spanish fluently; wife of Dale Jones.

She frequently drives the cars in which they travel, and in the battle with officers at Colorado Springs, Colorado, fired several shots with a revolver. Some two months ago she claimed to be pregnant, and it is possible she may be found at some maternity hospital.

Under the Postmaster General's "Notice of Reward," dated August 3, 1916, $1,000 is payable for information leading to the arrest and conviction of any person on the charge of robbing the mails while being conveyed in any car attached to a railway train, in violation of Section 197 of the Penal Code; however, the charge of MURDER pending against Dale Jones is the more serious offense, and he, with his wife, will be delivered to the authorities of the State of Colorado. The Commissioners of Colorado Springs, Colorado, have authorized the payment of a REWARD of $2,000, of which $1,500 will be paid for information leading to the arrest and conviction of Dale Jones, and $500 for information leading to the arrest and conviction of Margie Jones, his wife, upon the charge of the murder of Detective John Rowan.

Dale Jones and his wife, Margie Jones, are particularly desperate characters, and officers are cautioned to govern themselves accordingly when undertaking their apprehension.

Should either of these parties be located, their arrest should be caused immediately and the undersigned notified at once by telegraph.

JOE P. JOHNSTON,
Post Office Inspector in Charge,
Kansas City, Missouri.

KANSAS CITY, MO., NOV. 2, 1918.

H. D. HARPER,
Chief of Police,
Colorado Springs, Colorado

(10m)

78

# DEADLY GUNFIGHT AT COLORADO STATION

The gang of felons pulled in behind the old woman gassing her car at a filling station in Colorado Springs, Colorado. Little did the crooks know that the station's attendant had already made their identities.

All the attendant needed to do was play it cool. He watched the crooks add water to their car as he calmly took the old woman's cash, went inside, and dialed police.

John Rowan, chief of detectives, was first to get the call. He raced down the alley behind the service station, planning to cover the gang from the rear. Chief Harper and Officer Tom Shockley would counter, using their cruiser to block the gang's escape.

Rowan and his men rushed the vehicle. The officers ordered the felons to put their hands up. But one crook had a different plan, and he pulled a revolver and opened fire.

The bullets zipped through the air. Several lawmen dove behind the car while another, named Riley, ran for cover in the filling station. He emptied his revolver into the gang's car while Rowan doubled the fire.

The shooting bandit was struck and the gunfight looked to be over. Rowan approached the vehicle from the side, but his timing was bad. Margie Jones, the seventeen-year-old wife of gang leader Dale Jones, ran from the gas station, alerting her husband to the officer.

Jones spun in the front seat and fired point-blank into the approaching lawman. The bullet entered Rowan's right shoulder and left his body through his abdomen. Rowan fell to the ground, managing to fire off one last shot.

The bandits turned their attention to Riley. Not to be outdone, Riley returned fire, emptying his sawed-off repeating shotgun in a blaze of powder and smoke. He ran out of shells and switched to his revolver. But a well-placed bullet caught his hand, tearing off a finger. The shot knocked his pistol to the ground. The next bullet hit him squarely in the eye. Riley went down.

The old woman who had come for gas was frozen at the pump with fear, her windshield shattered by bullets. Henderson, the station attendant, ran through the barrage to start the old woman's car and drive the woman to safety.

With the path now cleared the gang sped off. Chief Harper and Officer Shockley fired desperately at the escaping gang. One round hit its mark, striking one of the passengers.

The band of criminals raced through the city's streets before the local fire chief picked up the chase in his roadster. The fire chief was unarmed but he kept pace with the crooks, that is, until engine trouble put him hopelessly out of the race.

The bandits had made their daring escape, leaving a mess of blood and gore in their wake. Rowan, their first victim, died en route to the hospital. A second bullet had struck his watch, stopping the timepiece at 3:10 p.m.

While Rowan was dead, Riley was holding on in poor condition. The brave lawman held a bullet lodged near his brain. One shot blasted off a finger and a third had hammered his foot.

The good guys found themselves on the ropes. But nobody knew how the gang had fared. It didn't matter; shocked at the brutality of the gunfight the citizens of Colorado Springs went out in force to hunt for the crooks.

"Five minutes after the shooting occurred, fully 200 Colorado Springs men, armed, were in search for the party," the *Colorado Springs Gazette* reported. "Within two hours after the shooting, every road leading from Colorado Springs was guarded, and every town within a radius of 100 miles had been notified and furnished with a description of the fleeing bandits."

Day four and the manhunt grew. Another officer was shot dead, bringing the tally to two. Detectives placed a "ring of steel" more than 100 miles in diameter around Colorado Springs. The ring of steel was nothing more than the weaponry of a growing vigilante force.

"There have been murder stories, tales of crimes as dastardly and as brutal as this, of wholesale slaughter by paid killers, but never in the history of Colorado has a murder narrative developed so quickly, broken from so many different angles, and finally resolved itself into so great a mystery as has the slaying of 'Johnny' Rowan and the vanishing murderers."

The tide would turn. First it was gangster Rod Sherrill, who police wounded in a running gunfight before taking into custody. Next it was Frank Lewis, a man detectives intercepted during a taxi ride to Denver.

Still, the two Joneses remained at large. A $2,000 bounty was placed upon their heads, raising the stakes to a new level.

Two months later, in November, the gun-wielding couple appeared at a Los Angeles filling station. This time police were ready. When lawmen rushed the couple's car, the felons pulled their pistols and opened fire. A lawman was the first to fall. The gunfire increased before officers finally delivered the two fatal bullets—one for husband and the other for wife.

The *Gazette* described the crime spree this way: "The stories of their escapades, their close scrapes with the police, their terrorizing and murderous plunder, reads like an extract from the most spectacular of dime novels and brings to mind once more the wildest night that Colorado Springs ever witnessed—a night when every man carried a gun: when there was talk of lynching and hanging: when [the] police department and civilians united in a chase and manhunt that covered [the] surrounding territory for a radius of 25 miles."

# WANTED

## PRESTON THAYER, alias WAIN

I hold Warrant for PRESTON THAYER, alias WAIN, charge MURDER.

Age 28, 5 feet and six inches tall, weight 160 pounds, medium dark hair and complexion, smooth face, limps badly in right leg. Light check coat, light stripe pants, light cowboy hat with brown leather band set with brass tacks, brown woolen shirt, carried large gun with yellow belt and scabbard, tan shoes. Arrest and wire

GEO. E. STONE,

Sheriff, Spokane Co., Wash.

# MURDER ON A FARM

There's no harm in a Tuesday morning handshake, or so Joseph Cechlovsky thought as he greeted the stranger on his porch that day in Ripley, Montana.

The Bohemian farmer asked his wife to make lunch for their unexpected guest. She complied, setting the meal on the table before moving off to feed the chickens in the coop.

When the poor woman returned from her daily chores, she found her husband dead on the floor, their guest gone, and their lunch untouched. The gruesome sight sent the woman into a panic. Horrified, she ran to find her son and inform the boy of the tragic news.

The boy set off at once to dial the Whitefish operator, who dialed the police, who summoned Lincoln County's top lawman. The sheriff was on the scene in no time flat, and news of the murder spread just as quickly.

"One of the most atrocious murders in the history of the state took place at Ripley at about noon today," the paper reported. "The motive was undoubtedly robbery, although nothing was taken from the person of the dead man."

The sheriff believed that the killer had tricked Cechlovsky into thinking they had met before. He further reasoned that the killer had struck Cechlovsky on the head with a nasty piece of stove wood measuring sixteen inches in length. The blow dazed the farmer, allowing the killer to stab him about the head and neck.

While the knife had gone missing, investigators found the bloodied stump of wood in the tinder box hidden behind the kitchen range. Hours later, a local station agent told the sheriff that he had sold a boarding pass to a suspicious fellow.

"Why was he suspicious?" the sheriff asked.

"Because he walked really fast," the agent said.

The sheriff didn't hesitate in cuffing a fast-walking man matching the description. But a good alibi prompted the man's immediate release. Walking fast wasn't a crime after all. A better description was needed.

"Mrs. Cechlovsky stated that the man looked to be about five-feet, five-inches in height, weighed about 150 pounds and seemed to have a red, smooth face," the paper reported. "He wore much-worn and dirty blue-bibbed overalls over the pants and wore a slouchy black hat."

A reward of $750 was posted for the arrest and conviction of Cechlovsky's killer. But the killer remained at large.

# $750
# REWARD

For Arrest and Conviction of the murderer of Joseph Cechlovsky, Sr., committed August 1, 1911, at about 12 o'clock noon

## DESCRIPTION OF MURDERER

About five feet five inches tall; wore dark colored suit with blue bib overalls on; black slouch hat; full red face; no beard; thick neck and heavy set and rather dirty looking

$500.00 of above reward will be paid by Jos. Cechlovsky, Jr., and $250.00 by the County Commissioners of Lincoln County

IN CASE OF ARREST NOTIFY ME AT ONCE

F. R. BANEY, SHERIFF, LIBBY, MONTANA

# $500 Reward

*Captured*

## Wanted for Murder

WALLACE, SHOSHONE COUNTY, IDAHO, SEPT. 7, 1912.

John Luoma, age 45; height 5 feet, 7 inches; weight 155; Finlander; light complection; sharp, round blue eyes; shaggy eyebrows; light brown hair, very thin; high, bald forehead; heavy light brown mustache; has short neck; has medium full face with about two weeks' growth of beard. He may shave clean to hide identity; has small blue scar on one side nose.

Walks with head up and shoulders slightly stooped; talks very broken English; is heavy drinker; occupation, miner, lumber jack and conducted a saloon in Spokane, Washington, in 1904; wears 7½ or 8 shoe; 36-30 trousers; when he left here on September 1st, 1912, wore brown trousers with brown stripe; gray coat and brown hat; high topped, brown shoes, that have been half-soled; has worked as miner in Arizona, Utah, Michigan, and lived eight years at Enaville, 20 miles northwest of Wallace, Idaho, where the murder was committed; he carried a 30-40 U. S. Winchester rifle; an open faced silver watch without chain; a black, rough handled jack knife with one broken blade, and a black handled razor; chews Peerless tobacco and some times uses snuff. Is a native of Wasa, Kauhajoki, Finland, and has relatives at Mesabe, Michigan. The County Commissioners of Shoshone County, Idaho, authorize the above reward for capture or information of his whereabouts resulting in capture of said John Luoma.

MICHAEL J. MAHER,
Sheriff of Shoshone County, Idaho.

*Picture taken 12 years ago, looks older now.*

WILLIAM J. BURNS,
PRESIDENT.
RAYMOND J. BURNS,
SEC'Y & TREAS.

TELEPHONE { HOME MAIN 6820
{ BELL MAIN 6820
NIGHT BELL EAST 1785

COUNSEL FOR THE AGENCY
JAMES M. BECK,
FORMERLY ASS'T U. S. ATTORNEY GENERAL.

CABLE ADDRESS: WILBURNS NEW YORK.

# THE WILLIAM J. BURNS
# INTERNATIONAL DETECTIVE AGENCY, INC.

NEW YORK, WOOLWORTH BLD'G.    CHICAGO,    FIRST NATIONAL BANK BLD'G.    LONDON, 5 REGENT ST. W.

ATLANTA,        EMPIRE LIFE BLD'G
BALTIMORE,      MUNSEY BLD'G
BOSTON,         201 DEVONSHIRE STREET
BUFFALO,        WHITE BLD'G
CLEVELAND,      ROCKEFELLER BLD'G
DENVER,         FIRST NATIONAL BANK BLD'G
DETROIT,        DIME SAVINGS BANK BLD'G
HOUSTON,        UNION NATIONAL BANK BLD'G
KANSAS CITY,    MIDLAND BLD'G
LOS ANGELES,    WALTER P. STORY BLD'G

REPRESENTING
AMERICAN BANKERS ASSOCIATION
AND
NATIONAL RETAIL DRY GOODS ASSOCIATION

415 MIDLAND BUILDING
KANSAS CITY. MO.

MINNEAPOLIS,    McKNIGHT BLD'G
NEW ORLEANS,    WHITNEY CENTRAL BLD'G
PHILADELPHIA,   STOCK EXCHANGE BLD'G
PITTSBURG,      COMMONWEALTH BLD'G
PORTLAND,       YEON BLD'G
SAN FRANCISCO,  FIRST NATIONAL BANK BLD'G
SEATTLE,        HINCKLEY BLD'G
ST. LOUIS,      FRISCO BLD'G
ST. PAUL,       NEW YORK LIFE BLD'G

MAKE ALL REMITTANCES AND ADDRESS
ALL COMMUNICATIONS DIRECT TO AGENCY

# $850.00 Reward

NAPOLEON B. VANN, *alias* "NIP" VANN

The Governor of the State of Kansas offers a reward of $100.00; Montgomery County, Kansas, offers $250.00 and the City of Caney, Kansas, $500.00, for the arrest and delivery to the proper authorities of Montgomery County, Kansas, Napoleon B. Vann, commonly known as "Nip" Vann.

This party is wanted for the murder of John H. McInroy, City Marshal of Caney, Kansas, who was shot and killed on the evening of November 12, 1913 in Caney by "Nip" Vann.

AGE—28 or 30 years.            COMPLEXION—Dark.
HEIGHT—6-feet.                 EYES—Dark.
WEIGHT—180 or 190 pounds.      HAIR—Black.
BUILD—Good.                    FACE—Smooth Shaven.
DRESS—Generally dresses like a cowboy, wears large white hat and boots.

## REMARKS

Vann is part Indian, carries himself erect, head up and moves in a nervous manner. He has taken part as an actor in a great many Wild West moving pictures and might secure employment from some Moving Picture concern.

Warrant is in the hands of R. W. Lewis, Sheriff, Independence, Kansas. Should any information be obtained concerning the whereabouts of Vann, same should be immediately wired or telephoned to our nearest Office or to the Sheriff at Independence, Kansas.

# THE WM. J. BURNS INTERNATIONAL DETECTIVE AGENCY, INC.
## 415 MIDLAND BLDG., KANSAS CITY, MO.

December 1, 1913.                            Either Telephone Main 6820

# GREAT NORTHERN TERROR

Harry Mathews and George E. Ball boarded the train and settled in amongst the passengers. Accompanied by a third man, they raised few suspicions as the train streaked across the Washington countryside.

But all wasn't well aboard train number 358, operated by the Great Northern Railroad. Mathews, Ball and their comrade had evil intentions, and when the moment was right they proceeded to rob and kill three passengers.

Job done, the killers jumped from the dynamo and vanished into the cold February night leaving behind few clues. The bloodhounds soon wailed as a posse of men began the hunt for the murderous band. Like lightning the killers had come and gone, pulling off a disappearing act that left investigators baffled and train passengers stunned.

The gang's ruthless nature fueled the law's desire for a quick arrest. The Great Northern Railroad was eager to capture the gang as well, placing $5,000 on the head of each man. Dead or alive was the order, just bring the killers in.

It wasn't long before the bounty increased to $30,000. That was $10,000 per head, not exactly small change. While the third man remained unidentified, the poster offered a clear likeness of Mathews and Ball—the latter a smarmy little fellow whose appearance sang of trouble.

Police were convinced that the three men had escaped into the forest. Maybe they had taken to the water in hopes of reaching the San Juan Islands? Bloodhounds picked up the scent, leading investigators to the tidal flats. The law was closing in—but it wasn't close enough. The clues ended at the water's edge.

"If any of the guilty parties are killed while resisting lawful arrest, the Great Northern Railroad Company will pay the reward—upon proof that the party killed participated in the murder and robbery," the railroad promised.

# $30,000 REWARD

**HARRY MATHEWS**          **GEORGE E. BALL**

The Great Northern Railway Company will pay a reward of Thirty Thousand Dollars ($30,000.00) for the arrest and conviction of the three men that committed the crimes of murder and robbery on Great Northern Train Number 358, between the stations of Burlington and Samish, Skagit County, Washington, on the night of February 20th, 1914, in case the capture of them shall be effected at the same time.

If any of the guilty parties are killed while resisting lawful arrest, the Great Northern Railway Company will pay the rewards above mentioned, upon proof that the party killed participated in the murders and robbery. Ten Thousand Dollars ($10,000.00) will be paid for arrest and conviction of each man.

## HARRY MATHEWS

Age, 26. Height, 5 feet 7 inches. Weight, 145 pounds. Build, medium. Complexion, dark and pale. Eyes, gray. Hair, brown, inclined to be coarse. Smooth face. Small round scar on back right hand. Scar one inch long on back right wrist. Has a fresh scar on palm of one of his hands. When last seen wore dark blue suit, black hat, like one worn in picture. Mathews served time in Montana State Prison, Deer Lodge, for Burglary. Mathews is wanted in Vancouver, B. C., for Burglary and attempting to kill a police officer while escaping. He is also wanted in Victoria, B. C., for Burglary and Highway Robbery. Also wanted in Edmonton, Alberta, for attempting to kill a police officer while escaping. He is also wanted at Thief River Falls, Minn., for sticking up and robbing Express Agent of Seven Thousand Five Hundred Dollars ($7,500.00). He is also wanted near San Francisco, Cal., for a $5,000.00 plume robbery.

## GEORGE E. BALL

Age, 25 years. Height, 5 feet 8 inches. Weight, 135 pounds. Complexion, light, pale. Eyes, gray. Hair, dark brown. Smooth face. Build, slender. Is a dope fiend. Wore, when last seen, a brown suit, black soft hat, like one shown in picture. Ball is wanted for Burglary and Highway Robbery at Victoria, B. C. He is also wanted at Vancouver, B. C., for Burglary.

Above photographs have been positively identified by ten different people. This, with other strong corroborative evidence, makes an exceedingly strong case against these men.

(THIRD MAN—Name and description not known.)

Any information concerning the past records of these two men will be highly appreciated.

All officers are warned not to take any chances in arresting these men as they are desperate criminals.

NOTE: If these men are arrested and convicted, the party giving information leading to above clew will be fully entitled to an equal share of the reward.

The terms enacted in this Circular will cancel all circulars and newspaper notices prior to this

# $300-REWARD-$300
## GERMAN COAL MINERS

Ellensburg, Wash., August 7, 191.

I am authorized by the Board of County Commissioners to offer a reward of $150 for the arrest and delivery to an office

On August 1, 1913, these men poisoned and robbed Kaspar Klaus, a fellow countryman. securing $180 and an open face gold watch, the numbers and make of which I am unable to give

I would suggest that you immediately take this matter up with the officers of all mines in your district and with your local postal authorities, as both these men correspond with friends and relatives in Germany. Both have followed mine work for several years and are unable to do any other kind of labor. If they are apprehended I would urge that they be separated immediately and not allowed to communicate with each other until a officer from this county arrives. Wire any information to this office collect.

## B. H. GERMAN. Sheriff.

# BETRAYED

Kaspar Klaus cashed his $180 paycheck and set out across Washington's beautiful Cascades to have a good time with his mining pals.

At his side were his two close friends and fellow immigrants, Rudolph Otten and Fred Dreshler. But little did Klaus know that his so-called buddies would become murdering fugitives, and that the good-timing trip would be the last of his short life.

Along the journey, young Klaus fell ill with a strange and sudden flu. Looking to help their sick comrade, Otten and Dreshler agreed to walk to the nearest town. After all, Easton was just up the road. They could locate a car, bring it back and give Klaus a ride.

As promised, the two men returned with the truck. They helped poor Klaus into the vehicle and, showing concern for his well being, took his $180 and gold watch for safe keeping.

Once in Easton the party checked into a hotel room. But Klaus' strange flu got even stranger. A doctor was needed and needed fast, and being the friends they were, Otten and Dreshler were the first to volunteer. They'd fetch the doctor personally.

The hours passed and the doctor never arrived. Neither did Otten and Dreshler. It was clear that Klaus had more than an upset stomach, and the doctor's delay concerned the hotel staff.

With their options running out, the employees tried convincing the ailing Klaus to go to the hospital. But Klaus refused. His friends, he insisted, would be back soon. His friends, he said, wouldn't leave him behind.

The night pressed on and the pain got worse.

Unable to watch any longer, hotel employees finally called for a doctor. The doctor, in turn, rushed Klaus to the hospital where attending physicians applied emergency medicine. Unfortunately for Klaus, it was too late. The damage was done.

It was clear that a crime had been committed and police were called to investigate. Klaus mumbled that the lawmen were mistaken. His friends would never poison him, let alone rob him.

Sure, Klaus mumbled, Otten and Dreshler were heavy drinkers and lazy workers, but that didn't make them lousy friends. Sure, he added, he had paid their fare to bring them to America. He even supported them from time to time after they arrived, but only when it became necessary.

Like the giving tree, Klaus had given his all. He even gave his gold watch and the last paycheck of his immigrant life. Four nights later he was dead.

Coroner A. J. Rose discovered the alarming truth: Young Klaus had been poisoned by strychnine. That meant murder and Otten and Dreshler stood out as the most likely suspects. What a shameless-looking pair these two were—Dreshler bearing a heavy mustache and a stiff black hat, while Otten looked out through beady eyes from his short, soft body.

Police stations throughout the Northwest and Canada received descriptions of the two men. No station was overlooked. A $300 reward was placed upon their heads. It was a fair bounty considering the betrayal they had played upon their closest friend—a man who had carried their dead weight until the very end.

# CRAZED WYOMING SHOOTER 👉

Working at the rail yard, Reynaldo Rivera didn't have Wyoming's highest-paying job. The Mexican immigrant needed cash fast.

So the sharp-dressed man did what any fellow would do and asked his pal, Federico Balensuela, for a $15 loan. But Balensuela wasn't in the mood to loan out his money, never realizing that by refusing he was making the last mistake of his life.

Talk was for the birds and the shots rang out. Rivera filled Balensuela with bullets and watched the man fall dead on the spot. Rivera then helped himself to the cash.

The *Rawlins Republican* was on the story, basing its news on "logical deductions" and "the most reliable sources available."

Antonio Luna was home with Balensuela that night. Once Rivera came knocking, it didn't take Luna long to sense trouble. While he turned to run, he didn't run fast enough. Rivera spun with light-ning speed and fired, hitting Luna in the back. Poor Luna crashed to the floor, unable to flee or call for help.

The law would have to reach deep to figure this one out. The descriptions given by the witnesses were sketchy. Most of them were too busy fleeing for their lives than to pay much attention to the shooter.

But investigators had their suspicions. They believed that Rivera had been in the home all along playing cards. The card game, they suggested, had gone horribly wrong.

Those who knew Rivera called him Chino. Here was a man fond of racy women, and "Mexican or Negro sporting women." For such a gigolo, police were confident they'd land their man in short order.

Still, officers had a hard time believing that robbery was part of his motive, "unless it happened in the game" of cards.

# $100 REWARD

*Lahru 1912*

## FOR REYNALDO RIVERA

---

## DESCRIPTION:

Age about 31; Weight 165; Height 5 ft. 6 ins.; Long curly hair, may be cut short now; was wearing mustache, may be smooth shaven; lips are thick like a negro; is a native of Old Mexico; wore brown striped suit; is a neat dresser and buys good clothing. Was working here in Round House for U. P. Ry. Roaming disposition, likely to be found around medium size towns; will hang around either Mexican or Negro sporting women. Is known by name of Chino among his acquaintances. Rivera held up a bunch of Mexican laborers, killing one and wounding another, and after robbing them of their money, left the town on the 19th of January, 1919.

Wire information to

A. A. SANDERS, Sheriff,
Rawlins, Wyoming.

# A SHEPHERD'S REVENGE

The two Wyoming shepherds stood toe to toe, ready to settle their grudge like men. But this was no ordinary grudge and it wouldn't end in ordinary fashion.

Like boxing champs, Albert Swartz and Frank Chavez came out swinging. Left hand, right hand, the dust stirred and the courage flowed as freely as the slanders. But all fights have a winner and Swartz proved to be the better man, soundly beating his 155-pound rival.

The fight was over and most men would admit to having been whipped. But Chavez carried a man-size chip on his shoulder and he couldn't let it go. Down but not out, the little Mexican grabbed a pistol from the bunkhouse, ready and willing to level the score.

Swartz saw it coming. He tackled Chavez and took the pistol, then beat him soundly for the lesson that was in it. Enough was enough and ranch hand Dick Hinkle finally stepped in to break it up.

"Knock it off," Hinkle barked, hoping cooler heads would prevail. "Now go on and wash up."

It was just as well. Swartz had had enough and the powerful shepherd waltzed off to check his horse. But Chavez had a different plan. He found Hinkle's rifle behind the bunkhouse door. Now, he thought, they would take him seriously.

They didn't have time to argue. The rifle cracked on the air and the bullet tore into Swartz's shoulder. The pain sent the wounded shepherd into an involuntary dance of pain. He clutched his shoulder and dashed behind the cabin. There, fearing Chavez was on his heels, Swartz circled the cabin in record time, only to reappear at the very spot where Chavez had first fired.

Chavez hadn't moved an inch. The madman simply waited for his victim to reappear and when he did, he fired again. Through the puff of smoke, Swartz stumbled against the bunkhouse. This time the lead tore cleanly through the man, opening a nasty hole in his chest. Three hours later Swartz was dead and Chavez was on the run.

"Mexican Kills Another," announced Wyoming's *Rawlins Republican*.

It was hardly headline news—that went to a local fish fry and barbeque celebration in Carbon County. Still, the papers would have their say.

"Chavez is nothing more nor less than a cold blooded murderer," the *Rawlins Republican* told its readers. "Every effort is being made to apprehend him."

Carbon County Sheriff Rubie Rivera was the right man for the job. He stood proud and rode fast and was hot on Chavez's trail. If Rivera guessed right, Chavez was heading south toward Colorado with the murder weapon and a box of ammunition.

Unfortunately, the fugitive shepherd could hide in the heavy timber indefinitely—that is until the weather or hunger forced him back into the waiting hands of lawmen. But lawmen would be waiting for a long time.

# $500 REWARD

For the arrest of FRANK CHAVEZ whose right name is SICILLO CHAVEZ, (Mexican), who murdered Albert Swartz on August 23rd, 1916, at Haug Park, Carbon County, Wyoming, and was trailed south to Jackson County, Colorado.   Chavez is very dark complexioned, may be taken for negro.   Has curly hair, dark eyes, somewhat bloodshot, thick lips, wears mustache, lower left lip hangs lower than right lower lip, as though it had been injured, hair slightly sprinkled with gray.   40 years of age, height 5 feet, 7½ inches, weight 155 pounds, wears 7½ shoe.   When last seen was wearing overalls and black hat.   Talks good English.   This man was headed south into Colorado.   Address all communication to

## RUBIE RIVERA.

SHERIFF CARBON COUNTY,

August 25, 1916.                                   RAWLINS, WYOMING.

# WANTED FOR MURDER
## AND SAFE BLOWING

## William Clay, alias Richard Dillon, Joseph Conroy

This man was recognized as one of the trio that blew the safe
in the Postoffice and killed the Night Watchman
at Rio Vista on August 29, 1914.

DESCRIPTION---Age, 38 years; Height, 5 feet 10¾ inches; Hair, dark brown; Complexion, medium dark; Eyes, light blue; Weight, 169 pounds.

TATOO MARKS---Clasped hands and rays on right fore arm.

REMARKS---Stout muscular build, long muscular arms, square shoulders, long features, small ears, low full forehead, small mouth, full eyes and good teeth.

Previous Prison Record--Folsom 4683, San Quentin 24915, Portland 1656, San Francisco 23124.

### BERTILLION MEASUREMENT

| IM 79.9 | IM 87.0 | 97.0 | 19.8 | 15.3 | 14.0 |
|---------|---------|------|------|------|------|
|         | 6.3     | 27.9 | 12.6 | 9.5  | 50.4 |

**FINGER PRINT CLASSIFICATION**

$$\frac{1 \quad u \quad I}{9 \quad u \quad 00} 10$$

## This man is wanted badly by this office.

### J. J. McDONALD, Sheriff,
### Solano County, Cal.

The charge blew the safe doors to the front of the Rio Vista, California, Post Office building, clearing the way to the loot inside. The cracksmen were in, the phone wires were cut, and nobody was around to stop them. The Post Office clock froze at 1:55 a.m.

Among the crooks was William Clay, a lanky man who wore a heavy mustache and stalked about with wide-open eyes. He and his villainous cohorts helped themselves to $300 and slipped away as easily as they came.

Just down the street the local marshal, J. P. Emigh, walked out the back door of his home for a late-night stroll. Known around the neighborhood as a brave and watchful guard, Emigh made his way toward the motion picture show where he might meet one of the city's finer residents. It would prove to be the last round of the watchman's honorable life.

"When he reached the end of the alley he is thought to have encountered a bandit stationed there as a lookout," the *Sacramento Bee* reported the next morning.

But no one had heard the safe blow open, and Emigh had not been warned of the crime. He paused on the street corner, not knowing he was standing face to face with a villain.

The brave marshal reached into his jacket for a piece of tobacco. He didn't have time to react before the crook blasted him once through the heart.

Only one resident claimed to hear the safe blow. This, the paper presumed, suggested that Emigh failed to hear the explosion as well, and was shot down without warning.

The dead officer was later found with that piece of tobacco clutched in his hand. The callous blast from the villain's gun electrified the city's police officers. The hunt was in full swing in no time flat.

Sheriff J. J. McDonald was on the case. He reasoned that the crooks had made their escape down the Sacramento River, either by foot or by boat. He would follow the river. He would also issue a warrant for the arrest of William Clay.

"This man is wanted badly by this office," the sheriff said.

# WHO SHOT SHERIFF SCOTT? 👉

Waving their guns in downtown Seattle, two bandits stopped cars and dragged passengers into the streets. The cowardly crooks accosted the motorists one by one, men and women alike. They corralled them like animals and forced them into a line, as if in a circus, and proceeded to march them down the street.

That's when the law arrived, sirens blaring. The deputies skidded to halt and jumped from their car—all except Deputy Sheriff R. C. Scott.

The unsuspecting lawman didn't stand a chance when the bullets rang out. Using their captives as a human shield, the villains fired away, killing Scott before he could climb from the car.

The gunmen were a cruel lot. They pushed their human shield forward and picked the pockets of the dead deputy. With the goods in hand they turned back for the car of Earl Eba—a man they had snatched from behind the wheel and paraded through the streets like a show dog.

But as the criminal pair made their retreat for Eba's car, the deputies finally got their chance to return fire. One bullet struck a bandit squarely in the chest, fatally wounding the cowardly man. The score was now even, but the match was far from over.

The unnamed robber made his getaway with his dead comrade at his side and the frightened Eba in the back seat. Once out of harm's way, the crook made a run for freedom. The manhunt was

on. Police began their shakedown by searching "all haunts of recognized narcotic addicts."

"The bandit at large is suspected of being a narcotic addict known to his associates as 'Blackie'," reported the *Seattle Daily Times*.

No one could say who, exactly, shot the deputy sheriff. An autopsy revealed that the lawman had succumbed to two .41-caliber bullets—the same caliber that killed the dead bandit.

One official theory suggested that the dead bandit had shot and killed Sheriff Scott, then accidentally shot and killed himself. The other theory held that Blackie shot his partner in crime with the guy's own gun, "either accidentally or purposefully," before tossing it away.

"'Blackie' is the only name the police have for the escaped man," the paper reported. "The escaped bandit is believed to have been wounded in the knee."

A man with a wounded knee couldn't hide long in Seattle without medical help. One man living off Seattle's underbelly—William Good—went to police and told them he had seen the notorious villain with the wounded knee. Apparently, the two had met each other in jail.

"He shook hands with me and said, 'Long time I no see you, either,'" Good told the press. "Well, I said to him, 'Where you bound?'"

Good told police that Blackie was off to the Bering Sea.

# $1,000 REWARD

## Wanted for the Murder of Deputy Sheriff
## R. C. Scott

### DESCRIPTION:

Age 32, Height 5 feet 8 inches, Complexion Dark, Weight 160, Wide Mouth, Round Face, Short Nose, Fast Walk, Short Neck, Square Shoulders, Lines Between Eyes over Nose, Uses Good English.

This man, name unknown to us, and his pal CADY, embarked on a wholesale robbery on the night of April 3, 1920.

Cady's PARTNER murdered Deputy Sheriff Scott, and later murdered Cady.

### Below is Cady's Picture---Who Is His Pal?

**CADY, THE DEAD BANDIT**
Cady was a drug addict. His partner is undoubtedly one too.

### Attention: Sheriffs, Police and all Peace Officers:

Look Cady's picture over carefully, perhaps you have handled him and his pal for whom we are now searching.

Arrest, hold and wire. Prompt action will be taken to extradite. The reward of $1,000 is offered by the commissioners of King County and will be paid for the arrest and conviction of the murderer.

## John Stringer, Sheriff, Seattle, Wash.

# $500 REWARD

## ═FOR THE APPREHENSION OF═

# HERBERT CAMPBELL
## Alias RYAN OR EVANS

# WANTED FOR MURDER

Five feet, 6-inches tall, weight 165 to 175, dark hair streaked with grey, week's growth grey beard, but face usually smooth; face--round large nose, dark blue eyes, slim built but pussy or big stomach. Dressed--black soft hat, coat light brown, figure invisible plaid, double breasted, three-button, top button missing, stitched around edge--tailors call invisible seam, size 38. Soft blue cotton shirt, black pants or blue overalls, patent leather shoes, took with him black cheviot dress overcoat, four button full length coat, this coat has label on inside right pocket giving date it was made, also name Harry Holland, and number of order, inside of right pocket, also label underneath collar, reading J. H. Holland & Co., tailors. This coat he will no doubt try to pawn. This man has followed circuses and claims to be a horse trainer. Also claims to be a prize fighter. The fellow is a hard boozer.
Arrest, hold and wire

# J. E. FERGUSON, Sheriff

## Chelan County, Wenatchee, Wash.

April 3, 1911

**RUBIE RIVERA, SHERIFF**

OFFICE OF

## SHERIFF OF CARBON COUNTY

RAWLINS, WYOMING

# $1,000 REWARD

## For BOB MELDRUM in any Jail in the United States

### DESCRIPTION:

48 years of age; weight 145 pounds; heighth 5 feet 8½ inches; medium complexion; full head of hair, mostly gray; dark blue eyes, well set in; deep creases around nose; teeth, all gold but three; two teeth upper left jaw and one lower left jaw are natural, very deaf and uses left ear mostly. When last seen was smooth shaven and wore grayish crusher cheap hat, dark coat and vest, grayish striped trousers, tan lace shoes and dark gray light weight overcoat.

**Wire all information to**

RUBIE RIVERA,
Sheriff Carbon County,
Rawlins, Wyoming.

Wanted for Murder..Neatly
dressed..Seen in Oklahoma City
Feb..19..1916. making for South
America but traveling slow..

MRS. LILLIAN AGNES ............... Weight about 100 pounds; ...ond; height, about five feet ... ...arge blue eyes and is very good l... ...out No. 2 shoe. W... ...wea... ...ng ring, and signet ring with "... ...ld watch and ...ain... the... ...was wearing a black dress, but... ...le or ... ...de. Also has whi... ...above... ...g black and white st... ...t T... ...little girl in Virginia City, Ne... ...MES F. MA...

Arrest... ...P. DONNE...

# IMMORAL PURPOSES

The U.S. Congress passed the Mann Act, poorly labeled the "White-Slave Traffic Act," in 1910 to help control prostitution. Now the federal offense of transporting women across state lines for immoral purposes joined the very short list of federal crimes: slavery, peonage, illegal immigration, crimes against federally chartered banks, antitrust actions, and land-transfer or bankruptcy fraud.

At once, county sheriffs, city police departments, and agents of the fledgling Bureau of Investigation realized the Mann Act was a great new tool. They could use it to go after any wanted criminal traveling with a woman who was not his wife—whether or not his reason for crossing state lines had anything to do with her. This same kind of creative thinking later led to Al Capone's being jailed for federal income tax evasion after he'd eluded answering for much more heinous crimes.

For county sheriffs, "white slavery" often meant getting the guy who had run off with someone else's wife. Transport, after all, was easier to prove than adultery—which was still a crime on the books. While women of marriageable age could thrill to the dime novels and "flickers" (silent films) that warned about naïve beauties tricked into lives of degradation by "white slavers," they could at least be reassured that if they were "seduced with false promises of marriage," the law was on their side. But woe be to the straying wife who left town with her lover!

# A FATHER'S VENGEANCE

What better way to celebrate Independence Day than to elope with your lover. With the promise of fireworks by night's end, it's hard to go wrong with a Fourth of July honeymoon.

Ynes Rodriguez, so young and pretty at seventeen, was looking for a little independence of her own. So with a nod and wink she ran off with her fiancé and elder lover, Juan Samillan, without saying as much as goodbye.

Whether she did it for love or as a demonstration of defiance didn't matter to her father, Ramon Rodriguez. He despised his daughter's suitor; one way or another, he swore to get the last laugh, vowing to see Samillan spend his honeymoon in the slammer.

"Youthful lovers put one over on dad," read the *Verde Copper News* of Jerome, Arizona. "The father is not inclined to forgive and forget."

Indeed he wasn't. Ramon swore to prosecute Samillan to the full extent of the law. He wasted no time placing a $100 reward upon Samillan's head, accusing him of something far more sinister than simply eloping.

"Arrest for White Slavery," was the charge.

Disparaging wanted posters were circulated, each painting the bridegroom in a less-than-flattering light. "Dark long face, thick lips, lower lip protruding down," the poster read. "Thick eyelids hanging down over eyes; very hairy over his body and has a very bestial appearance."

Ramon begged the help of police, and detectives complied, issuing a warrant for the couple's arrest. Lawmen were certain the lovers could be found among Spaniards in a boarding house or in a mining camp.

"One hundred dollars reward will be paid for their arrest and detention in any jail in the United States or Mexico," the warrant promised.

It was a tough price to pay for love.

# $100 REWARD!

## NOTICE TO SHERIFFS, MARSHALS AND THEIR DEPUTIES

**Arrest for White Slavery** Juan Samillan and Ynes Rodriguez, both natives of Spain, and wire at my expense when found to Ramon Rodriguez, Jerome, Arizona, or Joe Porterie, 24 Wall Street, Phoenix, Arizona.

**Description of Ynes Rodriguez:** Girl, 17 years old; Complexion, sandy hair, sandy eyes, gray blood spot on left eye lid; height, 5 feet; weight, 125 pounds. Good picture of the girl attached hereto. She was spirited away from her home by Juan Samillan July 4th, 1918, at Jerome, Arizona.

**Description of Juan Samillan:** Native of Spain; profession, miner; height, 6 feet; weight 170 pounds; complexion, dark eyes, dark long face, thick lips, lower lip protruding down; thick eye lids hanging down over eyes; very hairy over his body and has a very bestial appearance.

They may be found among Spaniards in a boarding house or Spanish hotel in some mining camp. One Hundred Dollars reward will be paid for their arrest and detention in any jail in the United States or Mexico. Wire at once when located. We hold warrant for their arrest.

# $25.00 REWARD

I hold a warrant for the arrest of one Frank Busz, wanted on a charge of adultery, and will pay the above reward for his apprehension.

This party is a minister of the Seventh Day Adventist denomination, and was at the time of his escape attending a campmeeting at Redfield, S. D. He may be found stopping with people of his church, if any in your locality. He leaves a wife and two children who may be following him.

Description as follows: Weight 150 lbs.; height 5 feet, 8 inches; light complexion; between 25 and 30 years of age; of German descent, but speaks good English; wore when last seen a dark coat, light pants and tan colored automobile cap; has gold crowned tooth in front.

Watch all Seventh Day Adventist meetings you know of in your locality, as he may be preaching.

Arrest and wire the undersigned—

## A. D. McRAY
### SHERIFF OF SANBORN COUNTY

Woonsocket, S. D., June 9, 1911.

---

6'9-'BER

# $25  REWARD  $25

I hold warrant for the arrest of one J. J. McMannes, charged with seduction, who left Greybull, Big Horn county, on or about Aug. 5th, 1915. Described as being about 35 years old, 5 ft. 11 in. or 6 ft. tall, dark complection, weight about 180 to 200 lbs. Has very heavy black eyebrows, extra good even teeth, very quiet, has worked for railroads in the capacity of roundhouse man and in oil fields, always wears dark clothing when dressed up. Is liable to be found in and about railroad works, machine shops, roundhouses, or even braking. If located arrest and wire at my expense.

B. F. WICKWIRE, Sheriff,

Basin, Wyoming.

J. O. MORTON, Under Sheriff. _
W. R. MARTIN, Deputy Sheriff.

I. E. SANFORD, Deputy Sheriff.
THOMAS KNUDSEN, Deputy Sheriff.

# Flathead County
## MONTANA

**SHERIFF'S OFFICE**
J. H. METCALF. SHERIFF.

KALISPELL, MONT..

*(Case Dismissed
Not Wanted)*

JUNE 20th, 1916.

I HOLD FELONY WARRANT FOR HALLY GRISWOLD FOR SEDUCTION UNDER A PROMISE

OF MARRIAGE.

     AGE THIRTY YEARS:WEIGHT 175 to 185#;SMOOTH FACE:BLUE EYES:DARK

RED OR AUBURN HAIR:HEIGHT 5' 9 or 10":SCAR ON BACK OF HAND:THINK IT IS THE

LEFT ONE:TEETH GOOD:STRAIGHT AND EXTRA LONG NOSE:USES TOBACCO IN ALL FORMS:

WEARS ABOUT A NUMBER SEVEN SHOE:USUALLY WEARS A BROWN SUIT:AT TIMES DRESSES

AS A LUMBER JACK:HAIR IS CURLY AND PARTS ON SIDE.

     ARREST AND WIRE AT MY EXPENSE.

     J.H.METCALF.

     SHERIFF OF FLATHEAD COUNTY.

NEVADA STATE POLICE

Office of
SUPERINTENDENT                                    Carson City, Nevada, October 7, 1913

# WANTED FOR WHITE SLAVERY

**ELMER COSGROVE.** Height about 6 feet 1 or 2 inches; hair, very dark brown; eyes, blue, and wandering; weight about 180 or 190 pounds. Is somewhat stoop-shouldered. Has a swaggering walk and loud voice. Always wears a soft hat, and when last seen wore a light Stetson hat and a very dark gray suit of clothes. Wears a No. 7 1-2 or 8 shoe. Is an inveterate cigar smoker. Makes a very good appearance when dressed up. Occupation, miner, but has followed bartending and has had experience as a teamster. Left wife and family in Virginia City, Nevada.

This man left Reno, Nevada, on train No. 3, on October 1, 1913. Reported seen in Sacramento, Cal., on the morning of October 2, with Mrs. Lillian Agnes Mahoney, whose description follows:

**MRS. LILLIAN AGNES MAHONEY.** Weight about 100 pounds; complexion, light; hair, blond; height, about five feet. Has large blue eyes and is very good looking. Has small feet; about No. 2 shoe. Was wearing wedding ring, and signet ring with "L. D." on it. Has also gold watch and chain. When last seen was wearing a black dress, but may be wearing a purple or brown velvet, which has short slit in the side. Also has white Albatros suit in which above picture was taken. Has been seen wearing black and white striped silk suit and large hat This woman left a husband and a little girl in Virginia City, Nevada.

JAMES F. MAHONEY.

Arrest, hold and wire. Warrant issued.

J. P. DONNELLEY,
Superintendent.

WAYNE ROGERS     GERTRUDE MAY PRATT     DORLESKA MAY PRATT
ELSWORTH PRATT

# I hold a warrant for the arrest of Wayne Rogers and Mrs. Gertrude May Pratt, for the crime of Adultery.

His Description:  22 years old, height 5 feet 7 or 8 inches, weight about 160 pounds, dark complectioned.  Smokes, chews and drinks.

Her Description:  Age 26, height 5 feet 6 inches, weight about 160 pounds, red hair a little fluffy, brown eyes.

They left Fort Dodge, Iowa. on Sunday night, September 22, 1912, taking 5 trunks, 3 new and 2 old, and two children, a girl and a boy----the girl is 9 years old and the boy 7, both have light hair.

Arrest and Wire Me at My Expense.

Very truly,

## R. S. LUND,

I. S. S. A.            Sheriff of Webster County, Iowa.

# PROMISE OF MARRIAGE 👉

When Robert Campbell met the sweet girl from Antioch, California, he was at once infatuated. The woman, only twenty years old, teased the thirty-six-year-old Campbell with her girlish features and dress, and that occasional charming wink.

By all accounts she looked to be a girl not yet seventeen. Yet the two quickly formed what the woman understood as an engagement. With her heart in knots she surrendered herself to her dapper fiancé. The problem was that Campbell's intentions weren't entirely honorable.

"She alleges that under promise of marriage Campbell committed the deed with which he is charged and then refused to not only marry the poor girl, but to have very little to do with her," reported the *Contra Costa Gazette*.

The woman filed her complaint with the district attorney's office. It was later agreed that Campbell would meet her, allowing the public prosecutor to serve as an intermediary by forcing the issue—either the marriage would take place or Campbell would go to jail.

As expected, Campbell never showed, leaving the woman scorned yet again. But when Campbell's brother sauntered in, the girl's curiosity piqued.

Campbell, the brother said, had every intention of showing, but he was stuck in a nearby town and wouldn't be able to make it.

The brother added that Campbell would be delighted to meet the woman on the 3:00 p.m. train to San Francisco if she'd be so kind to attend. Of course she'd attend, expecting marriage all the while, but Campbell still refused to follow through.

When the public defender got news of the story, he didn't delay in sending the local constable north to serve a warrant for Campbell's arrest. The man had dropped completely out of sight.

"His disappearance hangs as a black and menacing cloud," the paper reported. "He will be brought to [the prosecutor] to face this charge which is one of the most serious on the criminal calendar."

Campbell could run but he couldn't hide. Wanted posters bearing his likeness were posted far and wide. It seemed nobody liked a seducer. Witnesses reported seeing the man everywhere he went and it wasn't long before he fell into the arms of the law.

"The chief witness against him will be the girl whom he has betrayed and whose life he has ruined," reported the *Gazette*.

# IMPORTANT
## $100.00 Reward

**WANTED FOR SEDUCTION UNDER PROMISE OF MARRIAGE.**

ROBERT PAUL CAMPBELL: Height, 5 ft. 11 inches; smooth shaven; 36 years old; dark complexion; HAS A SCAR ON LEFT CHEEK, which has the appearance of being a burn, brown eyes; weight about 170 lbs; dimple in chin; soft peculiar voice; good set of teeth, at least one filled with gold; Grecian nose; stands erect; long fingers; back of hands reddish in color; very active; takes short steps; lifts feet quickly; habit of having hands in pockets; usually neatly dressed; when last seen here, had soft grey hat, grey suit of clothes, long grey overcoat; lace shoes; inclined to be sporty, usually drinks whiskey; he may be wearing an N. S. G. W. charm.

The large picture is a very good likeness of him.

I am very anxious to locate Robert Paul Campbell, and would ask that you make a special effort, and would appreciate any information given.

Disappeared from here about February 1st, 1911.

The above reward will be paid for information that will lead to his arrest and delivery to me.

R. R. VEALE, Sheriff,
Contra Costa County,
Martinez, California, U. S. A.

Dated, April 8th, 1911.

# $450.00 REWARD!

$50 Reward offered by J. Davenport and $200 by Jewell County, Kansas for the arrest of Ralph Simmons, and $200 by the State of Kansas for his arrest and conviction (arrest to be made within 90 days.)

(Sometimes gives name of Ray Smith.)

## DESCRIPTION:

Simmons is white, married, age 38, occupation barber and farmer. Weight 158 lbs., height 5 feet 11 inches; dark hair—straight. Wanted under white slave charge. Have warrant.

Lena Davenport, single, age 17 years, weight 120 lbs.; hair golden brown; dark eyes, straight; fair complexion. Parents ask detention. These two people last seen going east on Mo. Pac. R. R. from Concordia, Kansas, March 17, 1916. Home of both Mankato, Kansas. Telegraph immediately on locating them.       **D. W HENDERSON**, Sheriff,

Dated June 1, 1916.                                    **Mankato, Kansas.**

# Information
# WANTED

About the following described parties who are supposed to have left Sweet Grass, Montana, in Toole County, in company with each other about October 28th: 1917

| FRANK RUSH | Mrs. Richard Roscoe |
|---|---|
| Height 6 feet 1 inch | Height 5 feet |
| Age about 25 years | Weight 125 pound |
| Dark Eyes | Dark Brown Hair |
| Dark Wavey Hair | Dark Brown Eyes |
| Spanish Decent | Usually Dresses Well |
| Wore a Dark Suit and | Age 17 yr old, has been |
| Soft Hat | Married about 1 year. |

This office holds a warrant for the Arrest of Frank Rush on the charge of abduction. Address all Communications to      J. S. ALSUP,
Sheriff Toole County.

# $600.00 Reward

$100 ... ill be paid for the captu... ... Smith, alias John R. ... ...ed of bank robbery, ... ... from Sequoyah County... ...llisaw, Oklahoma, on Dec. 21... ... Description: White, weight 1... ...e between 50 and 60 ... ...10½ inches, eyes ... ...ay but has been ... ...mplexion usua... ...ustache, but ... ...st seen. Clai... ...hington but h... ...erokee count... ...year. This ... ...n to a rew... ...Gover-nor... ...very of Sm... ...e peniten-tia... ...Notify, ...NER, ...h County...

Jail Breaking, Army Desertion, Family
Abandonment, Assault, Whereabouts Unknown

# BE ON THE LOOKOUT

Railway trains had been blessing the West with greatly increased mobility and larger central cities for two to five decades, depending on location. Now, automobiles on the few passable roads were beginning to add to lawmen's headaches. Unfortunately, everyone could enjoy the blessings of disappearing in crowds or moving around the countryside quickly—including army deserters, escaped criminals, bullies, deadbeat dads, and just plain confused citizens. Thank goodness for wanted circulars!

# MISSING
## $50 Reward

For the Whereabouts of

# JAMES O'TOOLE

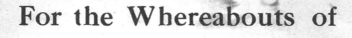

Disappeared from Butte, Montana on Nov. 30th, 1912. Nothing has been heard of him since. Age 51, height 5 feet 6½ inches, weight 140 pounds, eyes gray, hair dark, tinged with gray, tatooed blue star on left wrist; is a fireman and long-shoreman, worked for McCabe & Hamilton at Seattle, Washington.

This photo was taken in 1903, but is a very good likeness of him.

Wore a navy blue suit, solid gold watch, and chain, square locket made of quartz.

Wire or Write Information to

## Mrs. James O'Toole, 824 Colorado St.

or Montana Information Bureau, Butte, Montana.

# $200.00 REWARD

## WANTED FOR JAIL BREAKING

Alfred Eder and Charles Vaughan held here on a charge of Highway Robbery broke jail on the afternoon of April 5th.

| Description of Eder | | Description of Vaughan | |
| --- | --- | --- | --- |
| Age | 23 | Age | 21 |
| Weight | 180 lbs | Weight | 155lbs. |
| Height | 5ft. 10in. | Height | 5ft. 11in. |
| Hair | Light | Hair | Dark |
| Eyes | Blueish-Gray | Eyes | Dark |
| Complexion | Light | Complexion | Medium-Dark |

When they left jail Eder wore a pair of Tan Oxford Button Shoes, and Vaughan a pair of No. 9 special made Hanan Shoes, with rubber heels.

I will pay One Hundred ($100.00) Dollars reward for the arrest or any information leading to the arrest of either.

Wire any information at once to

**ROBERT H. PFEIL,**
**Sheriff of Shoshone County**

Press-Times Print, Wallace, Idaho.

# SPRING FEVER

In the fading light of a March afternoon, five prisoners suffering spring fever sprung themselves from the Lincoln County jail and slipped away into the coming night.

Some of the men were being held for breaking jail several months earlier. They only returned to the confines of their cell after their capture in Oregon.

The latest escape had been too easy for this motley band of burglars. They were seasoned pros and it would take something more foolproof than the Lincoln County jail to keep them locked inside, especially since they were waiting trial for their crimes.

"The old Lincoln County jail is a sore temptation to any prisoner to escape, judging from the ease with which they seem to exude through its walls," the *Shoshone Journal* lamented.

The paper didn't bite its tongue when stating its opinion. The reporter went so far as to suggest that the sign outside the jail, which warned passersby to stay out, should have had a complementary sign placed inside the jail, warning inmates to stay in.

But Edward Miller, Frank Sullivan, Frank Walsh, Joseph Hogan, and C. W. Darcy didn't want to stay in. None was a stranger to the penal system, each having spent his years in and out of prisons in the West. They had tasted freedom before and no rickety Idaho jail was going to hold them back.

So off they ran, carrying a lousy $50 bounty on each of their heads. Lawmen were told to use caution when making an arrest. They were undoubtedly some of the most slippery men in the region, maybe even dangerous, and they weren't going to go back to prison without a fight.

# $250.00
# REWARD!

$50.00 each for the arrest of the following described burglars, who broke jail at Shoshone, Idaho, at 6:30 p. m., March 27th, 1919. This is the second time they have escaped while waiting trial. They are without doubt five of the worst criminals in the country. Officers should be careful and take no chances with these men.

**EDWARD MILLER,** alias Edward Grautman, Dutch Miller. Police record Cheyenne, Wyo.; police record Billings, Mont., No. 905.

**DESCRIPTION.** American, age 30, height 5 feet 10½ inches; weight 170 lbs.; well built; brown hair, brown eyes, fair complexion. Part of left nostril gone.

**FINGER PRINT CLASSIFICATION:**

|  |  |  |  |
|---|---|---|---|
| 16 | U | 00 | 15 |
| 18 | U | 0 |  |

**FRANK SULLIVAN,** alias P. J. Milligan, Frank Needham, ex-convict Washington State Penitentiary, No. 6855, burglar; ex-convict Utah State Penitentiary, No. 2453, burglar; ex-convict Montana State Penitentiary, Deer Lodge, No. 5209; Dillon County, Mont., jail, petit larceny, sentence yet to serve, broke jail; police record Missoula, Mont., F. E. Murphy, No. 153; police record alias Frank Walsh, Cheyenne, Wyo.; police record alias J. J. Barrett, Deer Lodge, Mont.

**DESCRIPTION.** American, height 5 feet 9 inches; weight 165 lbs.; age 36, medium build, gray hair, blue eyes, light complexion.

**FINGER PRINT CLASSIFICATION:**

|  |  |  |  |
|---|---|---|---|
| 5 | U | 10 | 17 |
| 17 | U | 11 | 17 |

**FRANK WALSH,** alias Geo. Brown, Frank Carney, John Carney, Wm. McKonghan, alias Frank Barry. Platte County, Wyo., burglar, fugitive from justice, broke jail. Police record No. 365 Sacramento, Cal., vagrant; No. 32, Billings, Mont., selling liquor to Indians; No. 213, Butte, vagrant; Red Lodge, Mont., grand larceny; No. 1117, Dillen, 2 records, vagrancy, 6 mos., shooting railroad brakeman.

**DESCRIPTION.** American, age 42, height 6 feet, weight 162 lbs., medium build, hair slightly gray, blue eyes, light complexion, scar running from right side of mouth, 1 inch long.

**FINGER PRINT CLASSIFICATION:**

|  |  |  |  |
|---|---|---|---|
| 17 | I | 22 |  |
| 18 | 0 | 26 |  |

### Clipping Salt Lake Tribune.
## ALLEGED ROBBER GANG IS TAKEN

**Said to Be Responsible for Thefts Aggregating More Than $65,000.**

Special to the Tribune.

Shoshone, Ida., Sept. 17.— Through the arrest of Frank Edward Walch, Edward Miller, Frank Sullivan, J. P. Murphy and C. W. Darcy by Sheriff Wheeler of Lincoln county at Jerome a few days ago, it is believed that the boldest and most successful gang of burglars that has operated in this section of the country for years has been apprehended.

The evidence upon which the men were arrested was obtained by operatives of the Revelare secret service of Pocatello and Salt Lake City, personally directed by Luke S. May, head of the service. The quintet has been held to the district court under bonds of $5000 each and Chief May asserts that the past records of the men and the evidence which he has gathered will be sufficient to send them up for long terms.

Chief May announced today that information in his possession shows that Walch is wanted at Wheatland, Wyo., for breaking jail while being held on a burglary charge and that under aliases he has served sentences in Montana and California.

Edward Miller, Chief May says, has a police record at Billings, Mont., and Cheyenne, Wyo.

Frank Sullivan, according to Chief May, served a term in the Utah state prison for burglary, under the name of J. P. Milligan, and a term in the Washington state reformatory under the name of Frank Sullivan, in addition to serving time in the Washington penitentiary for burglary.

J. P. Murphy, the chief says, served a term of more than three years in the federal prison at Leavenworth, Kans., for breaking into a postoffice and also served a term in the Idaho state penitentiary for burglary.

C. W. Darcy is identified by Chief May as C. Weland, who served a term in the penitentiary at Walla, Walla, Wash., for burglary, and has a police record at Great Falls, Mont., as a shoplifter, under the name of C. W. Mitchell. Darcy also is charged with being a draft evader, as his prison record shows him to be only 29 years of age.

It is estimated by Chief

### Clipping Idaho Falls Register.
## BURGLAR GANG IN OPERATION IN THIS CITY

**Outfit Which Has Just Been Broken Up by Pocatello Secret Service Was Here**

**WORK WAS VERY SMOOTH**

**Many Merchants Did Not Know That Stores Had Been Burglarized.**

**Loot of More Than $70,000 Is Taken From Various Intermountain Merchants**

That Idaho Falls merchants may have suffered burglaries of which they knew nothing of because of the clever work of the thieves and that even now after checking up their goods they may find a shortage is brought out through the arrest of a gang of burglars who have been operating through this country.

It was L. S. May of the Revelare Secret Service of Pocatello that finally brought the gang into limbo. For some months he and his operatives have been working on the case and a number of times have been in this city, where the gang had headquarters in a local rooming house.

So smooth was their work that when a store had been robbed they would leave no trace of the work and many merchants whose goods have been identified had to be told of the inroads of the burglars before they knew of it. Officials of several counties arraigned for the service of Mr. May and his organization and from then on the result of the gang's working was unearthed.

May, who has been on the trail of the burglars for several months, and already has sent two of the gang to the penitentiary for long terms, that they have stolen more than $65,000 worth of merchandise in Idaho, Montana, Utah and Wyoming within the past eight months.

**JOSEPH HOGAN,** alias J. P. Murphy, Jos. Cosgrove, Sleepy Joe, Jos. Hamilton; ex-convict Idaho State Penitentiary No. 1704; burglar; ex-convict No. 9784-U.-S. Federal Penitentiary, Leavenworth, Postoffice burglar; police record all over country.

**DESCRIPTION.** Age 35, height 5 feet 5½ inches; weight 160 lbs., medium build, black hair, brokn eyes, dark complexion.

**FINGER PRINT CLASSIFICATION:**

|  |  |  |  |  |
|---|---|---|---|---|
| 28 | MI | 18 | REF. | 27 |
| 12 | OM |  |  | 12 |

**C. W. DARCY,** alias C. Weland, ex-convict Washington state Penitentiary, No. 5126, burglar; police record Colfax, Wash., alias C. Mitchell, alias Wm. C. Wesley; police record Roundup, Mont., larceny. Did not register 1917. Police record Great Falls, Mont., shop-lifting.

**DESCRIPTION.** American, age 30, height 5 feet 5¼ inches, weight 150 lbs., stocky build, black hair, brokn eyes, dark complexion.

**FINGER PRINT CLASSIFICATION:**

|  |  |  |  |
|---|---|---|---|
| 5 | R | 00 | 17 |
| 1 | U | 00 | 15 |

Any expense incurred in taking these men will gladly be paid by us. Send all information regarding them to Sheriff Wheeler, Lincoln County, Shoshone, Idaho, or to

# Revelare International Secret Service, Inc.
### Head Office, Pocatello, Idaho          L. S. MAY, Chief

# LOOK OUT FOR
# Escaped Prisoner and Stolen Horse!

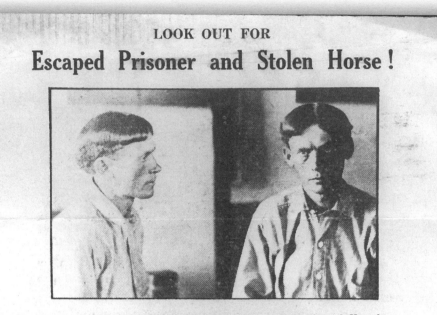

On the night of August 12th, 1914, the following described horse and saddle, the property of W. G. Armstrong, was stolen from his farm near Arcadia.

Blue Gray mare; weight about 900 pounds; branded A H M connected on right shoulder; mane has been recently roached; wire cut scar between knee and shoulder left fore leg; and was not shod.

Saddle was rather old and had what is known as a Montana fork; cotton cinch; old limber bit bridle had split ear head stall but split part was partly torn off.

Chas. S. Wheeler, whose photo appears above, escaped from the County Jail at Vale in the early morning of August 10th by sawing his way out with saws made from case knives, is suspected of this crime.

DESCRIPTION: Age 24; height about 5 feet 8 inches; weight about 140 pounds; dark auburn hair; fair complexion, but probably sunburned; slightly deaf.

His father and other relatives reside at American Falls, Idaho, and there seems to be no doubt but that he is going in that direction.

Officers please keep a close lookout for this man as he was being held on a felony charge and we want him badly.

Cancel our recent cards No. 6 S. C. Thompson and No. 7 Clarence Amis as they have been recaptured and returned.

Wire any and all information to me collect.

Dated at Vale, Oregon, this 15th day of August, 1914.

## D. H. KERFOOT, Sheriff.

# OFFICE OF THE SHERIFF OF KLICKITAT CO., WASH.

## GOLDENDALE, WASH., MAY 24, 1913

# Wanted for Abandonment of Wife and Four Minor Children Under Sixteen Years of Age

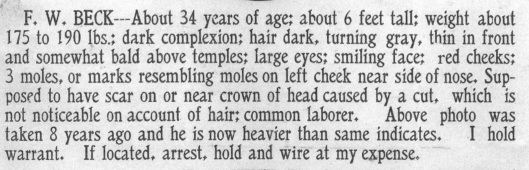

F. W. BECK---About 34 years of age; about 6 feet tall; weight about 175 to 190 lbs.; dark complexion; hair dark, turning gray, thin in front and somewhat bald above temples; large eyes; smiling face; red cheeks; 3 moles, or marks resembling moles on left cheek near side of nose. Supposed to have scar on or near crown of head caused by a cut, which is not noticeable on account of hair; common laborer.    Above photo was taken 8 years ago and he is now heavier than same indicates.    I hold warrant.   If located, arrest, hold and wire at my expense.

F. A. SMITH, Sheriff, Goldendale, Washington

# $50 REWARD EACH

## Will be paid for the capture of the following-described men, who are wanted by the Nevada State Police:

### LEWIS DELANEY (1929)

Age 20; weight 136; height 5 ft. 10¼ in.; hair light-chestnut; complexion light; beard sandy; build slender; occupation laborer; home Douglas, Wyoming.

Bertillon: 78.0 : 19.7 : 27.4 : 82.0 : 15.5 : 11.6 : 93.2 : 13.8 : 9.4 : 6.4 : 48.7

Finger-print : $\dfrac{1}{1} \dfrac{U}{Aa}$ 8

Delaney has no certificate of registration for draft service in the United States Army. He escaped from the Plymouth Ranch in Smith Valley while engaged in haying, on Sunday evening, July 8, 1917.

### ROY WELLS (1823)

Age 29; weight 162; height 5 ft. 8½ in.; hair red; complexion florid; beard red; build medium; occupation miner; home Seattle, Washington.

Bertillon: 74.1 : 19.3 : 27.1 : 83.0 : 15.3 : 12.0 : 92.2 : 14.1 : 9.6 : 7.4 : 49.3

Finger-print : $\dfrac{9}{17} \dfrac{R}{R} \dfrac{oI}{oI}$ 15

# Wanted for Jail Breaking

Broke jail on the night of July 25th,
1914, about 9:20 o'clock

## THOMAS KELLEY

age 38, about 5 feet 3 inches tall, weight about 130 pounds, hair sandy, eyes blue, slight build, sharp eyes, nose is long and broken, is twisted to the right side of his face.

Arrest and notify

F. R. BANEY, Sheriff,
Libby, Montana.

# $50.00 Reward

*Frank Rembert, Sr.*—Wanted for the murder of Ed. Hardwicke, on October 10th, 1910. Age 52 or 53 years, 5 feet 8 or 10 inches tall, weight 155 or 160 pounds, dark complexion, black hair, large black eyes. When last seen was wearing stubby black mustache, large mouth, prominent front teeth, short upper lip, has Southern accent and is very talkative, likely to appear very religious—a politician and claims to be wealthy. Has a brother in Pittsburg, Penn., a son in Idaho, two sons in Oklahoma and a daughter in Arkansas. Is a steel worker by trade and has worked in Alabama and Pennsylvania. Was a farmer in Texas. Has lived in Arkansas. Has bad rupture on one or maybe both sides and has recently undergone an operation for appendicitis. Chews tobacco. Right foot has been mashed. Escaped from custody at St. Louis, Mo., while enroute from Pennsylvania to Texas, January 4th, 1915. Will pay the above reward for him in any jail in the United States. Wire information to

## G. A. HAWKINS

January 23d, 1915.        Sheriff Wichita County, Texas

# SMOOTH TALKER WALKS FREE

The train pulled into the St. Louis, Missouri, station fifteen minutes too late, causing Sheriff G. A. Hawkins and his prisoner, Frank Rembert, to miss the southwest connection to Texas.

It was just as well. Hawkins wanted fresh air and his prisoner wanted to fill his medication. The pair had traveled together from Pittsburgh like two peas in a pod and it was a good chance for the both of them to get a look at the City of Blues.

So when Hawkins took the aging Rembert to fill his prescription at the local pharmacy, he couldn't have expected trouble. There was no need to handcuff Rembert. He wasn't going anywhere.

"I think I'll step back in the rear and wash up a bit," Rembert said while examining his filthy hands. "Pretty dirty for these big cities."

Hawkins didn't mind. The two had come a long way without trouble. So while the clerk counted out the pills, and while Rembert washed his hands, the sheriff turned to buy a cigar, looking to relax on the next train to Texas.

Hawkins found a dandy cigar. He tucked it in his shirt. But as he waited, delighting in the smell of fine tobacco, his prisoner slipped away.

"The drugstore opened into a saloon and it was through this he made his escape," Hawkins said.

Even with Rembert gone Hawkins wasn't overly alarmed. The old man had little more than $4 in his pocket and, while it was enough to leave St. Louis, he couldn't get far on it. His foot was mashed, he had just had an appendectomy, and he was old—hardly the qualities of man looking to remain at large.

Hawkins swore he didn't let Rembert go out of sympathy. But why didn't he handcuff him? After all, the prisoner was wanted for murder.

"Being of a retiring disposition and dreading city notoriety and the eyes of prying crowds, Hawkins decided not to handcuff Rembert," the *Wichita Daily Times* reported.

Besides, Hawkins argued, he had traveled with Rembert from Pittsburgh and the old man had proven to be cooperative if not downright charming. His southern etiquette was smooth and his words came fast. Cuffing him, Hawkins argued, would have gained the old man too much sympathy from the big-city crowds.

The joshing followed but Hawkins didn't care. He had lost $150 out of pocket for expenses and he didn't care about that either. But he did care about the loss of his prisoner. It doesn't pay to trust a killer.

"Hawkins said that he never hated anything so badly in his life as he did coming home without his man," the paper wrote.

# $100.00 REWARD

### For the Arrest and Delivery of
## CARL P. MACK

## An Escaped Convict

Carl P. Mack, alias James C. Clark, alias Roscoe Pound, alias James Fleming Wilson, alias Frederick McGuire, etc., who was serving a five year term in the United States penitentiary at Leavenworth Kansas, escaped from the custody of two of the Leavenworth penitentiary guards when riding on Northern Pacific train No. 41, near Sandpoint, Idaho, about 7 p. m., November 17, 1915. He was shackled with Leg Irons at the time of his escape, and it is thought probable took Northern Pacific train No. 4 Eastbound at Sandpoint on the early morning of November 18, 1915. The above pictures are good likenesses of Mack, who is described as follows:

### DESCRIPTION

Age, 38; height, 5 ft. 8¼ inches; weight, 155; build, medium; complexion, florid; hair, dark brown; eyes, brown.

Bertillon Measurements: 73.1, 77.0, 91.5, 18.0, 15.0, _____ 6.5, 25.6, 11.0, 8.9, 45.4

Postmasters and peace officers, particularly in Montana, will post this notice and make thorough search for this man. If he is apprehended hold him on a fugitive warrant and notify this office by telegram Government rate collect.

**CHARLES RIDDIFORD**
Post Office Inspector in Charge,
SPOKANE, WASH.

*Captured in Philadelphia*
*$200 Reward*
*See Fred McGuire in Circular under this*

# $50.00 REWARD

FOR THE ARREST AND DELIVERY OF

## CLAY M. LONG,

CHARGED WITH BEING A

## DESERTER FROM THE ARMY.

CLAY M. LONG, private, 77th Company, Coast Artillery Corps, who was enlisted February 1, 1915, for seven years, is reported to have deserted at Fort Barrancas, Fla., June 14, 1915. At enlistment he gave his residence as "U. S. Army," and the name and address of person to be notified in his behalf in case of emergency as Mrs. Kate Long (mother), 1624 S. Ninth Street, St. Joseph, Mo. Prior service: In 1912; residence Missoula, Mont.

DESCRIPTION (at date of enlistment): White; born in Daviess County, Mo.; age, 21¾ years; occupation, ranchman; eyes, blue; hair, light brown; complexion, medium fair; height, 5 feet 11 inches; weight 160 pounds. Prominent scars and marks: Front view—scar on right index finger, left ring finger, left knee and left leg; two scars on right knee. Back view—scar on left side of neck, each hand, and left leg.

A REWARD OF $50.00 is payable for the apprehension of this man, and for his delivery to the military authorities, until two years after the expiration of the period for which he was enlisted. The reward is payable at any United States Army post to any civil officer or other civilian who delivers the man there. If he is apprehended he should be delivered at, and the reward claimed at, the nearest Army post.

The act of Congress approved June 18, 1898, provides "That it shall be lawful for any civil officer having authority under the laws of the United States, or of any State, Territory, or District, to arrest offenders, to summarily arrest a deserter from the military service of the United States and deliver him into the custody of the military authority of the General Government."

Any information that may be secured as to the whereabouts of this man should be communicated to

### THE ADJUTANT GENERAL OF THE ARMY,

#### WASHINGTON, D. C.

June 30, 1915.                              24689

## Office of Sheriff, Kootenai County.

# JAIL BREAKERS

Coeur d'Alene, Idaho, Oct. 14th, 1911.

## TO ANY SHERIFF, CONSTABLE OR POLICE OFFICER:

# $50.00 REWARD

### Offered for each of the following parties.

## JOHN SUPPLE

A German, speaks good English, height 5 feet, 8 or 9 inches, reddish face and light hair, light mustache, straight nose, a new, reddish scar on forehead, dark clothes and light hat, when left. Fifty Dollars reward offered by the Sheriff of Kootenai County, Idaho.

## JESSE WHIPKEY

5 feet, 11 inches tall, 37 years of age, hair black inclined to be curly, heavy black eyebrows, Roman nose, wore gray trousers, black hat and black slippers when left, has quite a correspondence with women. Fifty Dollars offered by the Sheriff of Kootenai County. Whipkey is liable to correspond with Champlin & O'Marr, lawyers at Sheridan, Wyoming. Last worked at Mann & Hay Camp, near St. Maries, Idaho. By occupation he is a cook, painter and pimp.

# W. B. McFARLAND,
### Sheriff of Kootenai County, Idaho.

# REWARD

## $50 $50

BROKE JAIL AT THOMPSON FALLS, MONTANA, ON NIGHT OF SEPTEMBER 25TH 1911 BETWEEN THE HOURS OF 9 AND 11 O'CLOCK

J. C. ARMSTRONG, sentenced to seven years in state prison for Grand Larceny—Description: Age, about 30 to 35; height, about 5 ft., 7 or 8 inches; complexion, light; smooth shaven except for 3 or 4 days growth of beard; blue eyes; weight, about 155 pounds; has but one leg, left leg having been amputated about 5 inches below knee; wore a wooden peg leg painted dark color, wore a dark, soft hat; black coat and vest and dark gray pants; black soft shirt; glib talker; quite a cigarette smoker and chews tobbacco. Is probably accompanied by a boy by the name of

E. C. DRUM, who broke jail with Armstrong, and who was under sentence of one year instate prison for Grand Larceny.—Description: Age, about 20; rather slender build; height about 5 ft., 7 or 8 inches; weight about 140 lbs., smooth shaven; complexion, medium; brownish eyes and hair; hair cut short; has receeding forehead and head runs up somewhat to a peak; wore dark clothes; black soft hat; light soft shirt; black shoes; smokes cigarettes. If the two are found in company the older man will do the talking.

The above described persons were being held in the county jail, pending their removal to state prison, sentence having already been passed. The above reward of $50 will be paid for the apprehenson of the above described persons or a reward of $25 will be paid for either.

Arrest and hold them wherever found and wire me at my expense and I will send officer for them.

# WILLIAM MOSER

## SHERIFF OF SANDERS COUNTY, MONTANA.

## Address: Thompson Falls, Montana.

# $200.00 REWARD

For apprehension and delivery of Roy White to the officials of Butte county, South Dakota. Picture shown is good likeness. Further description as follows:

Age about 38 years, slender build, height about five feet, nine and one-half inches, weight about 155 pounds, black hair, inclined to be curly, parts it in the middle, slightly stoop shouldered, hard of hearing, upper front teeth quite prominent, two center upper teeth gold, one upper tooth missing, sharp features, good conversationalist, well posted horse man, also on horse brands.

**HI HANTZ,**

Sheriff Butte County,

Belle Fourche, S. D.

mar. 24, 1914

# WANTED---By U. S. Indian Dept.

Geo. Shaffer, 47 years old, weight 175 lbs., height 5 ft. 9 in., eyes dark grey, full; heavy sandy eyebrows, dark sandy brown hair, parted in middle; heavy red mustache, droops at corners; slim face, pointed chin, heavy beard if not shaved, bloodshot veins on high cheek bones, prominent nose, prominent teeth, uses tobacco freely, quiet, but has peculiarity in speech, like stammer and lisp; carries body erect, shoulders well thrown back, trade, cook, last at house of ill fame; rough dress, might be mark on arm, but can't describe it.   If found, arrest, hold and wire me at address on reverse side, or at Aberdeen, S. D.

BYRON McVEIGH,
Deputy Special, U. S. I. D.

August 4, 1914.

# $300.oo Reward

For Information   leading to the apprehension of Bert Goodwin, alias Bert Cue.  Age about 30 years, height 6 feet 2 inches, weight 210 lbs.  Has dark brown straight hair, brown eyes, one  a  shade lighter than the other, and eyes look  rather  sleepy.  Is  rather large boned, has quite prominent jaws, large mouth and full  lips, smooth shaved, good teeth, and used the  expression:  "I  reckon' and "You reckon" a good deal in his conversation.  Is quite a joker. Wore No. 10 shoe, and when last seen wore two pair  of  overal's, rather large, a double grey knt sweater, a brown necktie, a moleskin coat, sheep lined, a brown mixed cap.  Disappeared Apr'l 2, 1916.  Reward holds good until May 1, 1916.  Wire any information to

# C. E. Irwin
## Bowbells, North Dakota

# $50 REWARD

## FOR

# Information Leading to the Whereabouts of

# Jack McDonald

Left his home in Anaconda, Montana, October 21, 1914 and went to Butte. We believe that he is headed for Roseberg, Oregon. As he is without money we think he is walking. He has been insane at times for three years.

*Located in Butte*

DESCRIPTION: Age 48, height 5 feet, 10 inches, red complexion, grey eyes and light hair, slightly gray on top of head. Was clean shaved when he left home, and was dressed in a black suit and wore a black Fedora hat. He was also wearing a grey sweater with grey buttons, under his coat, and a soft white shirt. The only identification he had was 2 Eagle receipts of Aerie No. 18, and probably would not tell his name if asked. Deaf in left ear.

Anyone knowing his whereabouts or anything that would help to locate him,
## please notify

## JOHN BERKIN, Sheriff

**Silver Bow County,**                                            **Butte, Montana**

# $50.00 REWARD

_____

Marysville, March 15, 1916.

For information that will lead to the whereabouts of JOHN H. SADORUS, who disappeared from his home in Salt Lake City, Utah, March 20, 1915, after drawing his money from the McCormic Bank of that city.

The accompanying photograph is a good likeness of him. although taken several years ago. Description is as follows:

Age 60 years, height 5 feet 10 inches to 6 feet, weight 160 to 170 pounds, blue eyes, brown hair turning quite gray, occupation farmer and stock dealer. At the time of his disappearance Mr. Sadorus was in poor health, and it will be well to make inquiries at hospitals and coroners' offices.

This information is desired for the purpose of settling up the estate of his father who died at Sadorus, Illinois, October 13, 1915, and his sisters, Mrs. M. J. Bryden, Mrs. M. A. Brown of Marysville, and Mrs. S. F. Cope of Butte County, California, offer the above reward for any information that will enable them to communicate with him if living, or proof of his death.

If located notify either

MRS. M. J. BRYDEN,
516 D Street, Marysville, California

CHAS. J. McCOY,
Sheriff of Yuba County, California.

# $50.00 REWARD

### FOR THE ARREST AND DELIVERY OF

## WILLIAM J. ANDERSON,

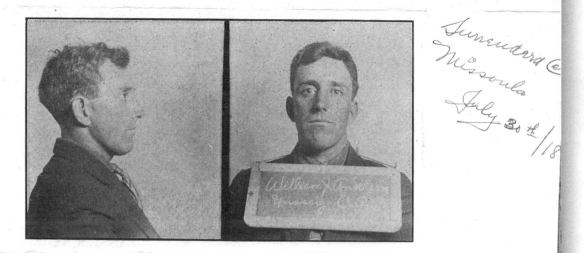

*Surrendered @
Missoula
July 30th /18*

### CHARGED WITH BEING A

## DESERTER FROM THE ARMY.

WILLIAM J. ANDERSON, 1st class private, Quartermaster Corps, who was enlisted November 22, 1913, for seven years, is reported to have deserted at Fort Snelling, Minn., June 3, 1914. At enlistment he gave his residence as R. F. D. No. 1, Missoula, Mont., and the name and address of person to be notified in his behalf in case of emergency as J. W. Anderson (father), R. F. D. No. 1, Missoula, Mont.

DESCRIPTION (at date of enlistment): White; born in Hastings, Minn.; age, 29½ years; occupation, carpenter; eyes, brown; hair, dark brown; complexion, dark; height, 5 feet 5 inches; weight, 125 pounds. Prominent scars and marks: Front view—vaccination scar on upper left arm; scar near center of forehead and on each knee; mole on right cheek and upper left arm. Back view—mole on upper left side of back.

A REWARD OF $50.00 is payable for the apprehension of this man, and for his delivery to the military authorities, until two years after the expiration of the period for which he was enlisted. The reward is payable at any United States Army post to any civil officer or other civilian who delivers the man there. If he is apprehended he should be delivered at, and the reward claimed at, the nearest Army post.

The act of Congress approved June 18, 1898, provides "That it shall be lawful for any civil officer having authority under the laws of the United States, or of any State, Territory, or District, to arrest offenders, to summarily arrest a deserter from the military service of the United States and deliver him into the custody of the military authority of the General Government."

Any information that may be secured as to the whereabouts of this man should be communicated to

### THE ADJUTANT GENERAL OF THE ARMY,

#### WASHINGTON, D. C.

June 19, 1914.                                    19989

# Escaped
# Prisoner

Henry L. Brown, age 36, appears younger, height 5 ft. 5 or 6 in., weight about 150 lbs., dark complected, brown eyes, black hair, black eye-brows and eye-lashes, good white teeth, one tooth missing, upper front, very noticeable; scar on upper *right* index finger, half of nail gone on this finger also.

Wore blue shirt, dark trousers and eight inch top logger shoes. This man is an I. W. W. and will associate with that class. Escaped from jail yard about 4:30, Wednesday evening, January 14, 1920.

Arrest, hold and wire.

W. F. Dunning, Sheriff,
Bonners Ferry, Idaho

# THE JAIL BREAK 👉

Inmate Tom French settled like a parrot upon the steel roof of his Pierce County, Washington, jail cell. He remained in place for several hours, waiting quietly for P. J. McCabe, the night jailer, to start his shift.

Meanwhile, the other inmates jammed George Pidd's lock with paper to slow the jailer down when he began making his rounds. When McCabe finally came on shift, Pidd went to work, calling the old jailer over to asked him to carry a letter to his wife.

"I have a note here I want you to send to my wife," Pidd said.

"This is no time to be sending notes to your wife," said McCabe.

French watched from the top of the cell. He looked down at the old-man jailer who never saw it coming. When the inmate jumped from his perch and swung a sock stuffed with a glass syrup bottle, the blow hit McCabe squarely in the head.

The jailbreak was on and several inmates cheered. Others took to the back of the cage not wanting to take part in the crime.

The old man grappled with French as best he could. But French was younger and stronger. He tossed the jailer to the floor like a sack of potatoes, beating him senseless with the sock and the now-broken bottle of syrup.

McCabe was out cold and Pidd went to work from inside his cell. He reached through the bars as a monkey for a banana and strapped the jailer to the bars. Other inmates joined in, gagging McCabe with cloth to leave him helpless and bleeding. They also took his .32-caliber Colt and the keys to the jail.

Working with French that wicked night was nineteen-year-old robber John Johnson and eight-een-year-old thief Arthur Grier. Toss in thirty-nine-year-old Sam Suddoth, who was serving time for vagrancy, and the gang of escapees emerged as a desperate lot.

But the inmates had a problem—they couldn't set Pidd free because of the paper jammed in his lock. Time was running out and the four men had to make their dash. They stole whatever they could carry, including $600 cash and the belongings of the other inmates. With their pockets stuffed they set into the night leaving Pidd behind.

The other inmates worked to free the wounded McCabe from his bonds. They carried him to the women's ward and told the matron of the crime. The matron sounded the alarm and the manhunt was on.

"The break was made after a murderous attack of night jailer P. J. McCabe, who lies today with his head cut and bandaged and his body shaking with the nervous collapse following his experience," reported Washington's *Tacoma Tribune*. "Posses of city and county officers are out scouring the country for a trace of the four escaped prisoners."

On the case was Marshal Hull. It was Hull who discovered the stolen car and convinced a logger to help him corner the dangerous men once they were spotted.

When French saw Hull and his men approach, he fired his stolen revolver with all his fury and the battle was on. The bullets rang out, sending the citizens of Kelso for cover.

In the end, Hull proved to be the superior marksmen. French reeled and fell as the marshal's lead bullet ripped into his flesh. With his partner down for the count, Johnson tossed up his hands. The two other inmates fled by automobile, making their narrow escape.

# WANTED FOR BREAKING JAIL

Please keep sharp lookout for the following described men who assaulted jailer and escaped from the Pierce County jail at 2 a. m. January 4th, 1918, and would like all efforts possible used for their capture:

## TOM FRENCH

Alias George Miller, American, 28 years, laborer, 165 pounds: 6 foot; brown eyes, brown hair; is an ex-convict from Walla Walla No. 6210; ex-convict out of Nevada State Penitentiary. Was just sentenced to Walla Walla, charge, burglary, five to fifteen years. Is a bad man. Has 32 calibre Colt's Automatic revolver.

## SAM SUDDOTH

American; 39 years; laborer; 5 foot 7 inches; 145 pounds; blue eyes, brown hair; received December 28th, 1917, and sentenced to six months for vagrancy.

## ARTHUR GRIER

American; 18 years; machinist, 5 foot 6 inches, 140 pounds; grey eyes; light brown hair; scar on left cheek bone; received December 28th, 1917, and sentenced to State Reformatory at Monroe for grand larceny.

## JOHN JOHNSON

American; 19 years; laborer; 5 foot 5 inches; 140 pounds; blue eyes; light hair; received December 28th, 1917, and held for robbery of postoffice committed at Cle Elum, Washington.

If located, arrest, hold and wire me and I will send officer.

**ROBERT LONGMIRE, Sheriff of Pierce County,**
**TACOMA, WASHINGTON**

January 4th, 1918.

*Captured in Canada.*

*Boise Pen*

# WANTED

## By the Sheriff of Shoshone County, Idaho for Jail Breaking, Saturday Night, October 11, 1913

## JESSE ANDERSON

AGE, 23; HEIGHT, 5 FT. 6 OR 7 IN.; WEIGHT, 155; HAIR, DARK; EYES, GRAY; COMPLEXION, MEDIUM LIGHT; HAS SMALL SCAR ON RIGHT CHEEK, JUST BELOW THE CHEEK BONE; ANOTHER SMALL SCAR JUST BELOW THE "ADAMS APPLE," CAUSED FROM REVOLVER SHOT. CONVICTED AND SENTENCED TO THE IDAHO STATE PENITENTIARY FOR FROM 1 TO 15 YEARS. CHARGE, BURGLARY.

*THOMAS McCABE, Sheriff, Wallace, Idaho*

# PORTLAND, OREGON, SEPTEMBER 11, 1911

# $25 REWARD

## ESCAPED FROM KELLY BUTTE
## NEAR THIS CITY, SEPTEMBER 9

## H. DEROSIER

Description as follows: Age 25 years; height 5 ft. 9 in., weight 165 lbs.; dark complected, smooth shaven, dark medium weight eye-brows, brown eyes that squint, slightly cross-eyed. Full round face, roman nose, right cheek somewhat swollen from toothache. Had trouble with left ear and had cotton in it. Lisps in talking. No tatoo marks or visible blemishes. Three fingers on left hand badly scalded on back, skin off and pretty raw from effects of burn. When last seen was wearing medium suit of clothes, patent leather shoes newly half soled and toe rubbers; wore brown derby hat. Talked of having friends in the vicinity of Salem, Oregon, but probably gone through Eastern Oregon. *If found, arrest, hold and wire at my expense.*

**R. L. STEVENS,** *Sheriff*

# $50 REWARD
## WANTED ESCAPED FROM ROAD GANG

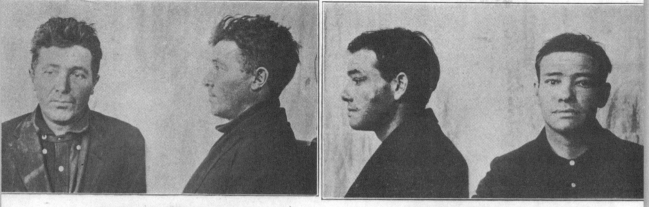

**GEORGE SHIELDS**          **WALTER BROWN, Alias DAVID LEATHAM**

## DESCRIPTION

George Shields, age 31, height 5-4 1-2 inches, weight 117, brown hair, blue eyes, medium complexion

Walter Brown, alias David Leatham, age 28, height 5-5 inches, weight 117, light brown hair, brown eyes, medium complexion, has a large boil on left side of face.

These two men escaped from county road camp. They are both professional thieves. I will pay a reward of $25.00 each for the arrest and detention of either of these two men.

Send all information to

# JOHN S. CORLESS

Sheriff of Salt Lake County, Utah

Dated at Salt Lake City, Sept. 15th, 1916.

# $50 - Reward - $50
## ESCAPE!

The following described Dr. C. Howard Childs, sawed out of the Multnomah County Jail on the night of June 15, 1916, at 4:45 P. M., and I wll pay the above reward for his apprehension and detention until an officer arrives for him.

**Dr. C. Howard Childs**

Name--DR. C. HOWARD CHILDS

Age - -     30 years
Height -    5' 8"
Weight -    135#
Eyes - -    Brown
Hair - -    Light Brown
Complexion-Sallow
Beard   -   Smooth Shaven

Features     Sharp; prominent cheek bones; slender prominent nose.

Scars and Marks - light pock marks on face.

Appearance-Looks like a "hop head."

Remarks -   Smokes Obak Cigarettes.

Clothes -   Will probably be wearing a salt and pepper Grayish-Brown suit. Will probably be wearing a Panama hat.

CRIME    -   Convicted of Obtaining Money by False Pretenses and sentenced to serve an indeterminate sentence of 1 to 5 years in Oregon State Penitentiary.

I also hold warrant for Mrs. C. Howard Childs, alias Helen Bly, alias Ruth Bly, alias Helen B. Bly, alias Nellie B. Laws, charging her with aiding C. Howard Childs by passing saws to him.   She is described as follows:

Age -  -    About 20
Height -    5' 6"
Weight -    115#
Hair -  -   Dark Brown
Eyes -  -   Large Brown
Build  -    Very Slender

Features-   Regular - Paints lips and cheeks.
Dress-  -   Wears Black Silk and Serge skirt.  Dark Bluish Waist - Black and white striped hat - Black high heel shoes.

These people will undoubtedly remain on the Coast and I would suggest that you cover the various hotels and apartment houses.

### T. M. HURLBURT

Portland, Oregon, June 17, '16.

Sheriff, Multnomah County.

# WYOMING JAIL BREAK

The two jailbirds spent long hours chiseling through eighteen inches of brick, using an iron rod torn from an army cot in their cell. Concealing their task with a pile of coal, all C. P. Hall and Roy Caldwell needed now was a signal.

And when the signal came, horse thieves Joe Bentley, Arthur Hill, and Glen Henderson joined the break. The five fugitives slipped on their bellies through the dog-size hole into the coal bins of city hall in Sheridan, Wyoming. From there, the escapees reached the furnace room. An unfastened door to the coal chute was all that stood in their way.

Hall, a balding, pipe-smoking thirty-four-year-old with a broken tooth, was in jail for burning down a non-unionized barbershop in Sheridan. Caldwell, in turn, was a thief and a large one at that. Investigators delighted in the problems he must have had squeezing through that hole.

But the jailers had some explaining to do and there was little time for jokes. They swore they heard nothing. The other prisoners, they said, gave no warning.

That was laughable, the prisoners said, presenting a different story. The four who stayed behind said they tried to alert the jailers by pounding on the steel door. Whatever the officers were doing, they didn't get the message.

"The prisoners frequently amuse themselves by singing and talking," one of the officers countered. "The prisoners must have framed their plot earlier in the day."

County authorities learned of the jailbreak at sunrise. A description of the missing men spread up and down the Burlington Northern line. Some said the men were heading for the hills. Others said no, they were heading north to Montana.

Wyoming lawmen saddled up for Montana to search for the escapees. The sheriff led the way, guessing that his thieves would go looking for horses. As expected, the horses turned up missing and the lawmen closed in on the hunt.

"Fugitives at Forsythe," the *Sheridan Post* declared. "Officers capture three of five who broke jail."

Hall and Caldwell remained at large. But the return of the missing horses—along with three of the five fugitives—was good enough to keep the media distracted.

"The recovery of the stolen horses is not the least pleasing feature of the capture, as the animals represented a considerable sum to the owner and their permanent loss would have been a severe blow," the paper reported.

**ESCAPED** from the Sheridan County Jail on the Night of August 17th, 1913, **FIVE PRISONERS** of the following description:

GLEN HENDERSON—Age 22 years, height 5 ft. 9½ in., brown hair, brown eyes, medium complexion, two upper teeth missing.

ARTHUR HILL—Age 23 years, height 5 ft. 7½ in., brown curly hair, blue eyes, dark complexion.

JOE BENTLEY—Age 18 years, height 5 ft. 8 in., blue eyes, very light hair, light complexion, good teeth, scar on right lower leg.

C. P. HALL—Age 34 years, height 5 ft. 6½ in., brown hair, brown eyes, medium complexion, one tooth broken off on right lower jaw, slightly bald on top of head, drinks and smokes a pipe.

Also ONE NEGRO—No description.

☞ Wire any information to

**RUSS M. HOOP**, Sheriff, Sheridan County, Wyo.

# $60 REWARD

## ESCAPED From United States Penitentiary Guard,
at Kansas City, Mo., Nov. 17, 1911.

## RICHARD J. LEWIS
.. ..No. 7356.....

Age 24, weight 117 lbs., 5 ft. 4 1-2 inches high, medium build, dark chestnut hair, maroon eyes, dark complexion, nose slightly bends to right, one upper and one lower front tooth missing, scar 1 1-2 x 1 in., at 3 in. below left elbow--outer, scar 1 in. obliquely across center right brow.

BERTILLON:—162., 170., 85., 18.3, 14.8, 13.5, 6.4, 25.4, 11.3, 8.6, 44.4.

Arrest and Wire

## R. W. McCLAUGHRY, Warden
## United States Penitentiary
### Leavenworth, Kansas

# $50
# REWARD
## WANTED FOR JAIL BREAKING
## SAT., JULY, 20, 1918
## JOHN KOKEL

Austrian; Age 27; Weight about 170; Height about 5ft 9inches; smooth shaven; dark complexion; brown eyes; black hair; combs hair pompadour; good teeth; upper lip short and shows teeth when smiling; very straight and well built; makes nice appearance. When he made his escape he was wearing a soft brown hat brown flannel shirt; blue overalls; black button shoes; has blue serge suit with him; will probably change clothes.

This man is a native of Austria and is registered in Lincoln Co. Idaho under serial number 475, order number 415, and is classified as an ENEMY ALIEN. Will probably claim nativity of some other country. Has taken out first papers at Kemmerer, Wyoming in 1912.

## WILL GIVE REWARD OF $50 FOR HIS ARREST
### NOTIFY CLARENCE WHEELER SHERIFF

JULY 22, 1918                    SHOSHONE, IDAHO

# YEGG-MEN BROKE JAIL
# $500.00
# REWARD EACH

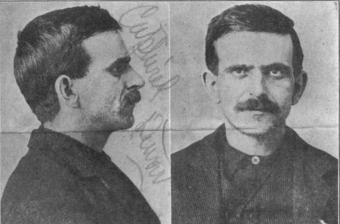

## NEAL MULCAHY

Alias, CON MULCAHY
" JAMES BRENNAN
" JAMES KELLY
" FRANK RYAN

Age 39 years, Weight 145 pounds, Height 5 feet 9 7/8 inches, Build Slender, Eyes Slate Blue, Hair Dark Chestnut, Complexion Light, Mustache Sandy, Nose Slightly Crooked, Little finger left hand amputated at 2nd joint. Vert, burn sear 2c at 8c above waist rear. Irregular blot scar 2 1/2c outer corner right eyebrow.

Bertillon Measurements. -77-2 - 90.0 - 92.2 - 19.4 15.5 - 13.3 - 7.1 - 27.3 - 12.6 - 9.5 - 50.2 = Finger Prints I R O O - 12 - 1 U O O

## DAN CARNEY

Alias, DAN MINNEN
" EDWARD L. BENNET
" LARANCE D. MAHONEY

Age 41 years, Height 5 feet 9 inches, Weight 145 pounds, Build Medium, Hair Dark Brown, Eyes Brown Complexion Sallow, Beard Brown, Very Heavy Eyebrows and Connected, Heavy Head of Hair, Smooth shaven, may grow Mustache. Right leg crushed, walks lame, 2 round scars on left forearm, scar on back of left hand. Mole on right side of face. Teeth upper front irregular.

## The Above Photos are a Good Likeness of Both Men.

MULCAHY and CARNEY were being held for burglarizing the Waterville State Bank at Waterville, Kansas, and the Beattie State Bank at Beattie, Kansas, both men have been convicted and sentenced to ten years each and would have been taken to the Penitentiary in a few days. $500.00 Reward will be paid for the arrest and delivery of each of these men to the Sheriff of Marshall County, Kansas. Arrest, Hold and Wire.

JAMES SULLIVAN, Sheriff,
Marshall County, Kansas

J. S. SEARLS, Special Agent,
Secret Service Bureau
State Banking Department
Topeka, Kansas.

# $100 REWARD

## UNITED STATES PENITENTIARY
## LEAVENWORTH, KANSAS

Escaped from Southwest Limited, C., M. & St. P. train, in vicinity of Moline, Illinois, April 13, 1914.

## AUGUST BRINKMAN, 8554

Alias Chas. P. Feine, Carl Rohl, Carl Bartels, Al Steinke, August Miller, Al Wilson, August Brink

Age 45, height 6 feet, weight 163 pounds, dark complexion, dark brown hair, dark brown eyes.

Small pit scar 5 inches above left wrist—rear; scar 3½ x ½ inches on rear of left elbow; second joint left middle finger slightly crushed; vertical scar ½ inch on first joint of right little finger—rear; small black mole 1½ inch to right of right corner of mouth.

Bertillion measurements: 182.5, 189.0, 93.0, 19.4, 16.4, 14.8, 6.9, 29.6, 13.3, 10.6, 51.7.

$100 REWARD will be paid for his delivery, after identification has been made, to an authorized officer of this Penitentiary.

Arrest and wire

**THOS. W. MORGAN, Warden**
U. S. Penitentiary, Leavenworth, Kans.

# $600.00 Reward

$100 Reward will be paid for the capture of John G. Smith, alias John R. Goodman, convicted of bank robbery, who escaped from Sequoyah County Jail at Sallisaw, Oklahoma, on Dec. 21st, 1918. Description: White, weight 155 pounds, age between 50 and 60 years, Height, 5 ft 10½ inches, eyes brown, hair turning gray but has been dyed brown, sallow complexion usually has heavy turned-up mustache, but was clean shaven when last seen. Claims to be from Seattle, Washington but has been near Cookson, Cherokee county, Oklahoma, for past year. This reward is offered in addition to a reward of $500 offered by the Governor of Oklahoma, for the delivery of Smith, alias Goodman, to the penitentiary at McAlester, Okla. Notify,

**B. F. FAULKNER,**
Sheriff of Sequoyah County,
Sallisaw, Oklahoma.

# $500 Reward!

## Arthur ~~~~~~~~~ alias Arthur Stanley

Description of man, ~~~~ picture: Age, 33 years; ~~~~ and 10 inches and 6 feet; ~~~~ pounds; dark hair, dark ~~~~ very prominent feature ~~~~ nose; rather thin or h~~~~ thinner than face sh~~~~ excessively. Is a ~~~~ graduate of the ~~~~ leans, and has b~~~~ in Fannin Cou~~~~ Texas. Wea~~~~ shoes, and d~~~~ shoes. Form~~~~ Louisiana; ~~~~ serted, livi~~~~ divorce fro~~~~ thinks she ~~~~

Descript~~~~ 125 to 13~~~~ complexio~~~~ ~~~~ and ~~~~

leaving Fort Worth green check suit and rathe~ small velvet hat.

$500.00 reward guaranteed for arrest of ma~ and delivery to proper officers. Wanted for em~ bezzlement, a felony, being a penitentiary offens~ under the laws of the State of Texas. Want gi~ held but not locked up; want her to have ever~ comfort and will pay any expense incurred ~ giving her proper comfort and attention, un~ officer can get to where she is under surveilanc~

This man might be engaged in his professio~ on any road work or construction work, and w~ make special request that thorough search b~ made of rooming houses and hotels.

From conversations had with friends, this ma~ ~ll probably be making his way to Central Amer~ ~ and officers at cities where steamers or frui~ ~rying boats or ships embark will confer ~ ~or if they will make investigation of ste~ ~ agents and ticket agents where this ~ ~ have purchased tickets for any Ce~ ~~~~ point, or any other point, and ~

Bank Robbery and Safe Cracking, Train Robbery,
Burglary, Robbery, Grand Larceny, Embezzlement,
Forgery, Obtaining Money Under False Pretenses

# TAKE THE MONEY
# AND RUN

**B**ank and train robberies—the signature crimes of the Old West in film and fiction—were spectacular if not all that frequent. The bad guys had plenty of other ways to get money without gambling on weather to bring in crops, taking on the dangers and miseries of underground mining, or enduring the six-day work week's boredom. The clean-handed crimes of embezzlement and forgery held highest status among the criminal class then, as they do now. They took intelligence, foresight, and impulse-control, qualities lacking or minimal in the average crook. Safecrackers—"yeggs" in contemporary slang—also ranked fairly highly, as did bunco (confidence) men. The former used specialized, delicate, mechanical skills, while the latter thought on their feet while manipulating victims' psyches to elicit greed.

What the "box" game in these posters is remains unclear. One kind of box used in cons was the faro box, from which cards were dealt while players bet on what card would come out next. The seeming game of chance wasn't one. Another box scam gulled victims into putting cash into a special box that could "scientifically" multiply its volume or increase the bills' denominations. In these posters, there is also mention of an up-to-the-minute con that used a plain envelope and new-fangled electricity in place of the changing box.

Boise, Idaho, Dec. 7, 1914

# WANTED FOR BURGLARY

# JAMES MEAGER
## Alias "BURNS"
## Alias "JAMES WILLIAMS

Age, 48 years; height, 5 ft. 8⅝ in.; weight, 175 lbs.; stocky build; hair brown "bald"; eyes, blue; complexion, ruddy; moustache, red; born in New York; occupation, miner. Was dressed in a dark suit of clothes; dark grey soft hat, size 7¼; new black shoes.

## BERTILLION

| Height | Head Length | L. Foot | Outer Arms | Head Width | L. Middle Fingers |
|---|---|---|---|---|---|
| 74.3 | 19.8 | 25.8 | 72 | 16.5 | 11.7 |
| Trunk | Cheek Width | L. Little Finger | R. Ear Length | L. Forearm | Trunk |
| 92 | 15.2 | 8.6 | 6.6 | 46.9 | 5-8⅝ |

Finger Print $\frac{9\ A0}{5\ A0}$ Ref. $\frac{9}{1}$     Discharged from I. S. P. Dec. 3, 1914.

Arrest and wire at my expense.   I hold warrant.

A. ROBINSON, Chief of Police.

# $1500 REWARD

## John Doe

45 years of age; 5 ft. 7 or eight inches tall; hair quite gray; two or three weeks growth of beard, sandy streaked with gray; wore about number eight shoe, middle finger of right hand missing; rather full face, wrinkled, high forehead; large, light blue eyes; weight about 145 lbs.; wore light khaki coat, pants darker and newer; gray flannel shirt; light hat, Stetson shape, pinched to peak at top, medium brim; smokes cigarettes; wore shirt unbuttoned at throat;

## Richard Doe

About 35 years of age; three weeks growth of beard, rather dark; hair brown; rather thin face; gray eyes; weight about 140 lbs; 5 feet 6 or 7 inches tall; wore tan khaki suit with norfolk coat; tan khaki or flannel shirt; 14 inch high top lace shoes, black; both men wore belts.

The two men above described, held up and robbed R. Boswell and son at the Boswell mine near Holland, Oregon, on the evening of May 2, 1918, securing about $6000.00 in gold. The gold consisted of three melted bars, two bars about seven inches long and one about five inches in length, some fine dust, a gold stick pin with six nuggets, five in the shape of a star with small nugget in center, gold ring Chinese design, engraved on inside of ring in Chinese characters.

**$500.00 will be paid for arrest and conviction of the above and $1000.00 for recovery of gold. I hold felony warrant, arrest and wire at my expense.**

### Geo. W. Lewis,
### Sheriff of Josephine County, Oregon.

# RAIL ROBBERS ESCAPE GUNFIRE

The two aging robbers clung to the railing on the Southern Pacific "Coaster" day train traveling from San Francisco to Chatsworth, California. When their masked heads finally appeared in the observation car, the passengers had a sinking feeling that something was wrong.

The bandits burst into the cabin brandishing silver revolvers and dastardly shotguns. Cries of alarm rolled through the car and the passengers rushed toward the head of the cabin.

Not everyone was able to escape the highwaymen. One robber moved forward, gathering members of the crew under the muzzle of his gun. He warned passengers to keep quiet and stay in their seats. He told them to keep their hands up and not to try anything funny.

As one robber kept watch, the other marched down the aisle, thrusting the loot into a sack slung at his side. Mr. Noback was out $70 and a gold watch. Mrs. Salat lost $8, a string of beads, and several rings made of gold, opals, and diamonds. The haul was getting big, but it could have been bigger.

"Many of the passengers saw the robbers or were warned of their approach in time to hastily conceal their money and valuables," reported the *Los Angeles Examiner*. "For this reason, the bandits failed in many instances to find anything but empty pockets, and the total sum of their loot was much less than it otherwise would have been."

The robbers told the conductor that any trickery on his part would result in instant death. The conductor had no reason to test the men's words.

He slowed the train as instructed and the bandits jumped off, toting their heavy sack of goods.

Others on the train weren't going to sit still and just watch the crooks fade away. A porter borrowed a shotgun for the occasion from a Wells Fargo messenger and gave chase. A railroad employee, along with several passengers, joined the hunt as well. It was a dangerous proposition.

"The bandits halted their flight long enough to empty both barrels of their shotgun and all the chambers of their revolver at the train," the paper reported. "The [posse] fired ten shots at the dim forms of the departing robbers."

The train chugged to Burbank where the conductor wired the police force in Los Angeles. A large emergency crew rushed to the scene. The police didn't hesitate in setting up roadblocks leading into the city, in addition to posting watches at strategic locations.

Questions followed. Were the two bandits actually members of the Ancient and Dishonorable Order of San Fernando Valley Train Robbers? The paper had its speculations.

"The plan of operation followed by the robbers is the same which has distinguished several other Southern Pacific train robberies," the paper reported. "It was just such a robbery that Sells and Sligh, the notorious robbers apprehended some months ago for the Harlow robbery, confessed, although there has always been doubt as to whether Sells and Sligh were really the robbers in that instance."

# $2000 Reward!

**THE SOUTHERN PACIFIC COMPANY** will pay a reward of $1000.00 each for information leading to the arrest and conviction of the two men who held up train 22, between Chatsworth and Hewitt, about 10:20 p.m., June 11th, 1915.

Following is best available description:-

### Number 1.

Ht. about 5 ft. 9 inches, weight 170-75 lbs., wore at the time of robbery an old soft black hat, dark colored coat, gray trousers, old shoes, black mask. Hands very rough and brown from sun. Voice abrupt and coarse. Carried sawed-off double barrel shotgun.

### Number 2.

Ht. about 5 ft. 7 inches, weight about 140 lbs., dark hair and stubby mustache both streaked with gray. Wore Scotch plaid cap, blue bib overalls, black mask and glasses at time of robbery. Voice heavy, quick, and determined. Hands rough and brown from sun. Carried Colt automatic revolver.

Robbed passengers and crew of various sums in cash, jewelry, etc., as follows:-

Check $30.91 signed by J. B. Noser, check $13.17 signed by Laugenbreck-Hown, Arroyo Grande.

Two gold watches, one with metal fob.

16 size, 17 jewel Elgin watch, case No. 7520804, works No. 13710234. Monogram on back in old English "E. R. A."

Gold beads, gold ring with one opal and two diamonds.

Double Eagle Consistory ring, name "R. H. Smith" and date "1903" inside.

Signet ring, initials "S. B. S."

Gunmetal case, alarm watch, mkd. "F. S." with diamonds.

Gold chain, knife attached, enamelled gold scarf pin.

Locket, mkd. "F. S." with diamonds.

Purse containing papers and checks, F. Shearer, and two gold cuff buttons with diamonds taken out.

Traveller's checks, R. H. Wright on East Pittsburg National Bank.

Two and one half R. R. tickets, Denver to San Diego.

Any information regarding same should be forwarded immediately to J. C. Cline, Sheriff, Los Angeles, C. E. Sebastian, Chief of Police, Los Angeles, or to the undersigned.

**M. T. BOWLER**
*Chief Special Agent S. P. Co.*
Room 325 Pacific Electric Bldg.
Los Angeles, California

# WANTED FOR FORGERY

Red Lodge, Montana, August 9, 1913

J. L. GRAY, union printer; height 5 ft. 8 or 9 in; weight 170, rather fleshy; about 32 years old; has scar on left side of nose; dark hair, brown eyes, small hands and arms, wears No. 8 shoe.

Left here July 28, wearing blue trousers, gray coat, soft shirt, black shoes; was smooth shaven. Smokes cigarettes. Likely to be found in the company of lewd women. If located, arrest and hold at my expense. I hold warrant.

**W. H. GEBO, Sheriff, Red Lodge, Mont.**

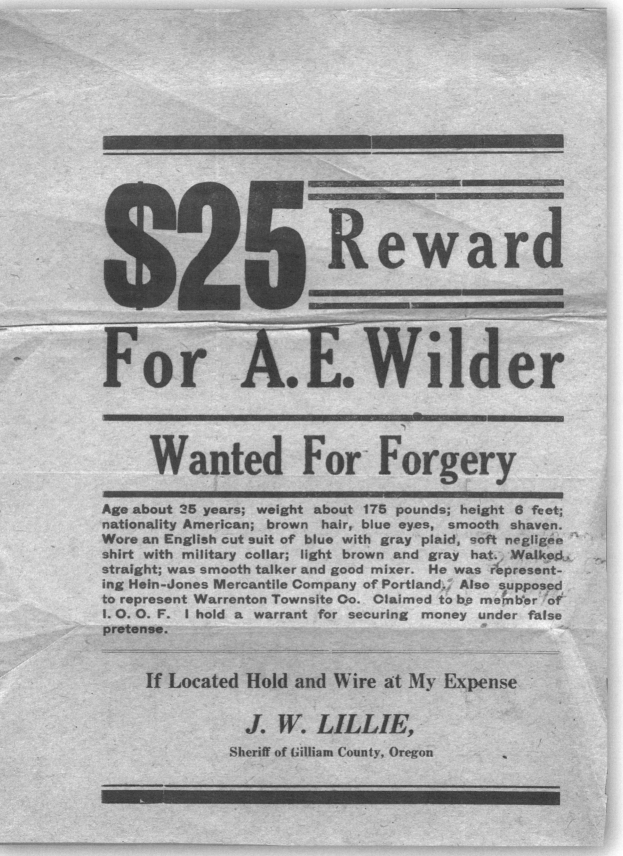

# $25 Reward

## For A.E. Wilder

## Wanted For Forgery

Age about 35 years; weight about 175 pounds; height 6 feet; nationality American; brown hair, blue eyes, smooth shaven. Wore an English cut suit of blue with gray plaid, soft negligee shirt with military collar; light brown and gray hat. Walked straight; was smooth talker and good mixer. He was representing Hein-Jones Mercantile Company of Portland. Also supposed to represent Warrenton Townsite Co. Claimed to be member of I. O. O. F. I hold a warrant for securing money under false pretense.

### If Located Hold and Wire at My Expense

### J. W. LILLIE,

**Sheriff of Gilliam County, Oregon**

# THE MAN WHO WOULDN'T DIE 👉

As the train whistle blew in the bustling downtown district in Missoula, Montana, Vernon Garlick stood tall and proud behind his bar, passing spirits off on the regulars at the Brunswick Saloon.

But this St. Patrick's Day wouldn't end in blasé fashion, and by night's end, Vernon's stubborn ways would become his only saving grace.

The evening turned ugly when two thugs entered the popular downtown pub, their faces hidden by handkerchiefs. Their strange masquerade was a sure sign they were up to no good.

"Hands UP!" they ordered.

The command took the bar patrons by surprise. The men didn't wait to argue. They raised their hands, leaving their drinks on the bar.

But Garlick figured the heist was more likely a St. Patrick's Day joke than a petty robbery. So the Irishman reached for his gun, intending to show the two masked men that he hadn't missed the point of their pleasantries.

And so it happened that Garlick turned, gun in hand, and the bandits fired. It wasn't a joke after all. The bullet struck the bartender keenly in the hand, knocking his revolver to the counter. Still, Garlick took the weapon in his good hand and returned fire.

The shot was on the mark. It hit one thug in the arm. Garlick readied the pistol to fire again. But before he could release another round he was hit squarely in the chest. This time it was serious. The Irishman clutched his chest, stammered, and fell.

"I'm done for, boys," he uttered.

Garlick fell and the bandits fired four more times. Gunsmoke filled the pub, screening the crooks as they made their daring escape. One bar patron snatched up Garlick's blood-slick gun. He reached the door only to see the crooks streak into the alley. He fired once and missed as the hold-ups vanished into the dark.

"Vernon is Doomed," the Saturday headlines read. "Bartender fatally wounded by unknown pair."

Hospital surgeons said that even Garlick's superb nerve couldn't pull him through. It wasn't a good sign for the Irishman, and while he fought for his life, the city's lawmen spread their dragnet.

The district had come to life and two men were on the run, one of them wounded in the arm. Police were confident they'd make a quick arrest. Officers searched departing trains and hauled men from the city's dark alleys for cross-examination.

At Garlick's bedside was Deputy County Attorney Paul Dormblaser. He pressed Garlick on the details of the crime. It wasn't long before the Irishman confessed—yes, he knew the two men who peppered him with bullets, but, no, he wouldn't give their names.

"I have an idea," Garlick said. "But I don't care whether you get them or not. They didn't get me. Not by a long shot."

Sunday came and detectives continued their

*Brunswick Bar Holdups.*  Missoula, Mont, 3-18-1916

Wanted for Holdup and attempted Murder, No-2, Age 20, Height 5-2, Weight 135-40, Smooth Face, Dark Complexion, Dark Hair. Piercing Black Eyes, Sharp Features, Sharp Nose, and shows some Indian Blood, Wears dark suit, with Overalls that are torn at bottom, red and Balck check Mackinaw. Dark Cap.

These boys held up a saloon here last evening and party shot atis not expected to recover, and may have in their possession 45 Cal Revolver and one of smaller caliber, also heavy Gold Watch of Foreign Make, 21 Jewels:

Kindly advise all of your Deputies to be on the lookout for these men, if located arrest hold and wire my expense.

R.J. Whitaker, Sheriff.

search, suggesting they had uncovered "new and more definite clues." Meanwhile, Garlick held his tongue, baffling the public, the police, and the press with his ability to cling to life.

"Surgeons operated on him and after extracting three bullets managed to check for flow of blood," the *Daily Missoulian* reported. "It is thought now that Garlick has an even chance of recovery."

The weeks passed, the fugitives remained at large, and Garlick made his reappearance.

"Those of his friends who saw him could scarcely believe their eyes," the paper said. "When they told the story to others they were looked upon as untruthful men."

# $500 Reward!

## Arthur Stanley Covell, Alias Arthur Stanley

Description of man, of which the above is a picture: Age, 33 years; height, between 5 feet and 10 inches and 6 feet; weight, 150 to 160 pounds; dark hair, dark eyes, red complexion, very prominent features, especially prominent nose; rather thin or hatchet faced, considerably thinner than face shown in picture; smokes cigars excessively. Is a Civil Engineer by profession, graduate of the Tulane University of New Orleans, and has been working on road construction in Fannin County, with headquarters at Bonham, Texas. Wears light suit, dark hat and dark shoes, and dark blue suit, with light hat and light shoes. Formerly lived at 523 Seguin St., Algiers, Louisiana; his wife and children, whom he deserted, living there now; he has never obtained divorce from wife. Is traveling with girl, who thinks she is married to him but is not.

Description of girl: Age, 20 years; weight, 125 to 130 pounds; dark hair, hazel eyes, rosy complexion; very attractive; has scar about one inch and half long on left side of neck, quite noticeable unless collar is worn. Wore when leaving Fort Worth green check suit and rather small velvet hat.

$500.00 reward guaranteed for arrest of man and delivery to proper officers. Wanted for embezzlement, a felony, being a penitentiary offense under the laws of the State of Texas. Want girl held but not locked up; want her to have every comfort and will pay any expense incurred in giving her proper comfort and attention, until officer can get to where she is under surveilance.

This man might be engaged in his profession on any road work or construction work, and we make special request that thorough search be made of rooming houses and hotels.

From conversations had with friends, this man will probably be making his way to Central America and officers at cities where steamers or fruit-carrying boats or ships embark will confer a favor if they will make investigation of steamship agents and ticket agents where this man may have purchased tickets for any Central American point, or any other point, and to keep a lookout for him in the future.

If arrested, notify

## CULLEN BAILEY, Chief of Police, Fort Worth, Tarrant County, Texas.

## W. E. BIGGERSTAFF, Sheriff, Bonham, Fannin County, Texas.

## NACE MANN, Sheriff, Fort Worth, Tarrant County, Texas.

# $200 REWARD

Louis Parodi.                    Ector Oppicini.

## DESCRIPTION.

**Louis Parodi**—Age, 36; height, 5 feet 1¾ inches; weight, 156 pounds; hazel eyes; black hair; nationality, Italian; small growth resembling cows horn on second joint left ring finger; vertical scars, three on first and second joints right thumb.

**Ector Oppicini**—Age, 30; height, 5 feet 4¼ inches; weight, 179 pounds; eyes, light blue; black hair; nationality, Italian; two dim scars near center forehead; top of right ear gulped, small piece out.

---

## These men are notorious Bunko men, and use the "BOX GAME"

---

John Glezos of this city offers a reward of $100.00 each, for their arrest and detention until officer arrives and 10 per cent of all money recovered of $5,000.00 taken.  Arrest and wire at my expense.

JOHN S. CORLESS,
Sheriff Salt Lake County,
Salt Lake City, Utah.

July 8, 1915

# Wanted
## For GRAND
## LARCENY

And Obtaining Money Under False Pretenses

---

W. T. Harris

Height 5 foot 10 inches

Weight 160 pounds

Hair light brown

Wore a blue serge suit

And Mackinaw Coat

---

Charged with stealing a load of flax and a team of heavy horses and wagon. Selling the flax at Sunburst, Montana, to the Sunburst Mercantile Company and receiving therefore $30.00 in cash and a check of $98.84. The payment on the check has been stopped. This man tried to get the check cashed in Great Falls at hotels and s loons but was unsuccessful. Kindly notify parties interested. I hold a warrant for this man's arrest. If apprehended wire me.

J. S. ALSUP, Sheriff, Shelby, Montana.

# WANTED

## FOR

## Grand Larceny and Attempted Rape

# JIM WARD

## Alias EDWARD LONG

Age, about 32; height, about five feet nine inches; eyes, blue; high cheek bones; weight, about 160 pounds; hair, dark; light complexion; smooth shaven. Marks: Three bullet wounds upper part of body.

When last seen, was wearing overalls, brown coat and brown cap. Had considerable money, and may change wearing apparel.

I hold warrants charging grand larceny and attempted rape.

**$50 REWARD.** Board of County Commissioners have authorized payment of the above stated reward for the arrest and conviction of Jim Ward. In this case conviction is certain. Arrest and notify

## D. E. GRAY, Sheriff

Dated, Bozeman, Mont., Nov. 1, 1915.

# Wanted for Grand Larceny

## $25.00 REWARD

# GEORGE TILLMAN

**DESCRIPTION AS FOLLOWS:** Weight 160 pounds; age 26 years; hair light blonde, light complexioned; occupation miner; height 5 feet 8 inches; slender build; blue eyes; smooth shaven; has a tattoo on back of right hand of an anchor done in blue color. When last seen he wore a brown suit and brown hat with dented top, also a light colored stock collar. Hair was rather long. Is very quiet and unassuming.

This man is supposed to have left here on the morning of March 12, 1912, after robbing his room-mate of $159.00.

Wire any information, my expense. The above reward will be paid for his arrest until an officer can arrive with proper papers for him.

## CHAS. G. SMITH,

### Chief of Police,

### TONOPAH, NEV.

# THE QUIETEST THIEF

George Tillman was the lowest kind of thief. The quiet and unassuming man, who was fond of his dented hat and brown suit, didn't ask the question of what friends were for, but rather, how much were his friends worth.

In the case of his roommate, pal, and fellow miner Tom McGilligan, the answer was $159.

Tillman had worked in the Nevada cities of Tonopah and Goldfield for nearly two years, yet nobody knew much about the quiet man of short stature. And while he dug gold from the arid hills by day, he had barely a penny to his name.

So when Tillman became restless, people noticed. He wasn't the kind of man to confide in others. But he did mention from time to time how he'd like to go away, somewhere exotic.

Those that knew Tillman said his sentiment to escape was fueled by a letter he received from a young woman. Her lovely picture adorned the dresser in his room.

"It was understood that Tillman, before he came West, had been in the Navy, as many of his expressions were those of a man who had followed the sea," the *Tonopah Daily Bonanza* wrote. "The police learned today that the fugitive had an anchor tattooed on his right hand."

Police issued a regional bulletin for a man with a tattoo. A $25 reward was offered in California, Utah, Washington, Oregon, and Arizona. Police secured many promising clues and spread their dragnet with "such thoroughness that the early capture of Tillman is practically an assured fact."

Nevada's finest appeared confident, but then again, they always did.

"We have an excellent description of Tillman and we have wired the officers of a number of cities, and I expect that we will have him in custody before long," said Tonopah's assistant police chief.

"There are several clues which we have secured this morning that greatly encourage us," the chief added. "But I don't care at the present time to say what they are."

# $100.00 REWARD

## For the Arrest of
## Robert (Bob) Splaine

Age 38, height 5 feet 10 inches, weight 175 lbs., well built, nationality American. Dark brown hair, dark complexion, large square jaw, two vaccine scars on left arm, one on right, upper front tooth gold capped. Several scars on back of neck from boils. Had a growth at one time on first finger of right hand.

*I hold warrant for Grand Larceny. If arrested, hold and wire at my expense.*

### HARRY E. STARK,
*Sheriff of Okanogan County, Okanogan, Washington.*

Independent Print, Okanogan, Wash.

*Refound Burke returning to*
*Pueblo Col*

*Sent to Pen 6 years*

# $500.00 REWARD

**will be paid for the return of jewelry stolen from the residence of J. A. Thatcher on Saturday night, February 3d, 1912, described as follows:**

1 Pair of Solitaire Diamond Ear Rings.  1 Scroll Diamond Pin with 11 stones (extra large stones).  1 Round Pin set with medium sized diamonds.  1 Solitaire Diamond Ring, large stone (gentleman's ring).  1 Ring Marquoise Setting, emerald in center and surrounded with diamonds (modern cut stones).  1 Ring Cluster Setting Square Emerald surrounded with medium sized diamonds (modern cut stones).  1 Ring large Ruby and large Diamond Stones set diagonal, large stones.  1 Ring with five diamonds set across the finger, large one in center, two graduating off on either side. Tiffany style mounting.  1 Round Pin set with 8 large opals, 8 small diamonds and 8 small emeralds.  1 Medallion Pin surrounded with large whole pearls and small diamonds.  1 Pin Fresh Water Pearls, set in shape of a daisy with one tiny diamond dew drop.  1 Carved Necklace set with pear shaped amethyst.  1 Pair Gold Nose Glasses and pin, engraved M. A. T., and round pin and chain with automatic spring.  1 Ladies Leather Hand Purse, 4 inches long; had cards and papers and also contained a brand new $10.00 bill and some silver.  1 Necklace set with green stones (12 or more stones).  1 Long Gold Fan Chain, heavy links.  All articles except where otherwise noted, are of old-fashioned design.  Give information at once to

## DENNY McDERMOT, Chief of Police

February 6, 1912.                                                                 PUEBLO, COLORADO

# ARREST!

## CHESTER CANTREL

27 or 28 years old, weigh about 165 lbs., rather dark muddy complexion, light brown curly hair, thick and heavy, parts in the center and grows rather low on forehead; large blue shinny eyes hasa large sharp Roman nose, very high in center, protruding mouth, sharp face, pointed chin, **TEETH ON UNDER JAW**

**RUN TO A POINT LIKE A GOPHER'S,** back of jaw prominent and heavy. Cheek bones medium high, talks fast with Southern accent, twitches muscles at base of jaw when working and not talking.

HE IS A SMOOTH TALKER, AND WILL TRY TO MAKE YOU BELIEVE HE IS NOT THE MAN Wanted He Looks Pleasant and Good Humored.

## He is a Painter by trade and Drinks.

## Claims to be from Arkansas.

# He is Wanted for Forgery

Left Wibaux September the 18th.
He was wearing **Blue Striped Overalls, a Blue Coat and New White Shirt with Black pencil strip,** tie to match, new heavy **dark tan Shoes, No. 7 1-2 or 8, speckled cap**

LATET News says he stole a $25 Blue Serge Suit, with West Allis, Milwaukee, Wis., on inside pocket and he may be wearing that.

We think he bought a Small Soft Black Stetson Hat with a Wide Band and with E. F. Peterson, Wibaux, Mont., on the Sweat Band and will be wearing that instead of the cap.

He obtained about $80 in Cash through forged Checks, when he left here.

ARREST AND WIRE ANY INFORMATION AT MY EXPENSE,
J. W. JONES, Sheriff Wibaux,
Wibaux County; Montana.

P. S. Kindly hand to your deputies, or Police.

# WANTED

## FOR OBTAINING MONEY ON FORGED DRAFT

### CHINOOK, MONT., MAR 21st. 1913

I hold warrant for the arrest for L. C. Sanders alias J. A. Wilmott, alias Geo. W. Nelson, alias C. A. Morrison, alias J. C. Adams.

The above party cashed a forged Draft here for $100.00, drawn on the AMERICAN NATIONAL BANK OF LOUISVILLE, KENTUCKY, on March 4th, 1913, made payable to L.D. Saunders and drawn or claimed to have been drawn or issued by OLD KENTUCKY DISTILLERY by M. W. Hallandery, Secretary and Treasurer. The checks or drafts are bogus, uses a regular printed draft form; checks are numbered and protectograph used. Will have some business house indorse draft for him.

I am advised that such checks have been passed in California, Oregon, and Montana, and used the above names as payees:

## Discriptions of the above party are as follows

Age about 40,      Height 5 feet 6 inches
Weight about 150 lbs.    Complection, Dark
Hair Dark,           Jewish Nose
Has right eye Peculiar or Defected
Decayed or colored front teeth
Wore Black Derby Hat

Smooth talker, and claimed to have been raised in Kentucky, and will inquire at banks as to who are responsible saloon keepers. When he left here started on west bound train.

Any information wire at my expense, and if found arrest and I will come after him.

I. A. NEIBAUR, Sheriff.
By J. H. MIEWALD, Under Sheriff.

## Office of J. K. Smith, Sheriff Sonoma Co., Santa Rosa, Cal.

Card No. 93, Second Issue.                    February 28, 1913.

# WANTED FOR FORGERY

### THOMAS T. MARTIN

Waiter by occupation, age 32, weight about 135; smooth shaven; short build; **left shoulder lower than the right, which is quite perceptible**. Is quite a lady's man. Arrest and notify. **Watch eating houses, hotels and restaurants.**

J. K. SMITH, Sheriff.

FORM 88-5M-1-20-'14
WILLIAM J. BURNS,
PRESIDENT.
RAYMOND J. BURNS,
SEC'Y & TREAS.

COUNSEL FOR THE AGENCY
JAMES M. BECK,
FORMERLY ASS'T U.S. ATTORNEY GENERAL.

PHONE SUTTER 1775

CABLE ADDRESS: WILBURNS NEW YORK.

# THE WILLIAM J. BURNS
# INTERNATIONAL DETECTIVE AGENCY, Inc.

NEW YORK, WOOLWORTH BLD'G     CHICAGO, FIRST NATIONAL BANK BLD'G     LONDON, 5 REGENT ST. W

BIRMINGHAM, BROWN-MARX BLD G.
BALTIMORE, MUNSEY BLD'G
BOSTON, 201 DEVONSHIRE STREET
BUFFALO, WHITE BLD'G
CLEVELAND, ROCKEFELLER BLD'G
DENVER, FIRST NATIONAL BANK BLD'G
DETROIT, DIME SAVINGS BANK BLD'G
HOUSTON, UNION NATIONAL BANK BLD'G
KANSAS CITY, MIDLAND BLD'G
LOS ANGELES, WALTER P. STORY BLD'G

REPRESENTING
AMERICAN BANKERS ASSOCIATION
AND
NATIONAL RETAIL DRY GOODS ASSOCIATION

**800 FIRST NATIONAL BANK BUILDING
SAN FRANCISCO, CAL.**

MINNEAPOLIS, McKNIGHT BLD'G
NEW ORLEANS, WHITNEY CENTRAL BLD'G
PHILADELPHIA, STOCK EXCHANGE BLD'G
PITTSBURG, COMMONWEALTH BLD'G
PORTLAND, YEON BLD'G
SAN FRANCISCO, FIRST NATIONAL BANK BLD'G
SEATTLE, HINCKLEY BLD'G
ST. LOUIS, FRISCO BLD'G
ST. PAUL, NEW YORK LIFE BLD'G

MAKE ALL REMITTANCES AND ADDRESS
ALL COMMUNICATIONS DIRECT TO AGENCY.

July 13, 1915

# $50.00 REWARD $50.00

**ONE GOLD RING,**
Setting: One sapphire and two diamonds in platinum.

**ONE GOLD RING,**
Setting: Small sapphire surrounded with rose diamonds, platinum setting.

**ONE PAIR DIAMOND EAR-RINGS,**
Old style heavy gold setting, fasten with clasp.

**ONE PAIR DIAMOND EAR-RINGS,**
Hoop style. Set one-half in diamonds, one half in sapphires. No fastenings.

**ONE LARGE DIAMOND PIN,**
Crescent shape; platinum setting.

**ONE LADIES PIN,**
Small bird set with diamonds.

**LADIES BROOCH,**
White enamel, small diamond in center.

**ONE GENTLEMENS STICK PIN,**
Design: A fox; set with small diamonds.

**ONE GENTLEMENS STICK PIN,**
Design: Horse Shoe. Set with pearls.

**ONE BRACELET,**
Diamond and platinum; diamonds one half way round.

**ONE BRACELET,**
Diamond and pearl; set in platinum.

**ONE BRACELET,**
Moorish design; with jade screw. Imitation gold.

**ONE LARGE GOLD MESH BAG,**
Mirror inside; sapphire clasp; flat mesh wrist chain; small sapphire in a slide on wrist chain; tassell with seed pearls on bottom of bag; purchased at Tiffany's.

**ONE SMALL GOLD MESH PURSE,**
About four inches square.

**TWO GOLD POWDER BOXES;**
**ONE ST JOSEPH'S MEDAL;**
**ONE GOLD BALL;** all attached to chain.

We are authorized to pay the above reward for the return of the jewelry herein described (no questions asked) which was stolen from a residence in San Francisco, California on Thursday, July 8th, 1915.

Address all communications to the nearest office of:

## The William J. Burns International Detective Agency, Inc.

PINKERTON'S BANK & BANKERS' PROTECTION
BY

# PINKERTON'S NATIONAL DETECTIVE AGENCY.

Founded by ALLAN PINKERTON 1850.

**WM. A. PINKERTON,** Chicago. } Principals.  **ALLAN PINKERTON,** New York.  **GEO. D. BANGS,** General Manager, New York.

—OFFICES—

| | | | | | | |
|---|---|---|---|---|---|---|
| NEW YORK | 92 Liberty Street | PHILADELPHIA | 112-116 North Broad St. | CHICAGO | 127 South Fifth Avenue | SAN FRANCISCO | Flood Building |
| BUFFALO | Fidelity Building | RICHMOND | Times-Dispatch Building | CINCINNATI | Mercantile Library Building | DENVER | Foster Building |
| SYRACUSE | Onondaga Co. Sav. Bank B'ldg | ATLANTA | Candler Building | INDIANAPOLIS | Merchants Bank Building | SALT LAKE | Kearns Building |
| TORONTO | Manning Chambers | NEW ORLEANS | Hibernia Bank Building | ST. PAUL | Capitol Bank Building | LOS ANGELES | Wilcox Building |
| BOSTON | 77 Franklin Street | HOUSTON | Chronicle Building | WINNIPEG | McArthur Building | SEATTLE | Alaska Building |
| HARTFORD | Hartford Nat'l Bank B'ldg | PITTSBURGH | Benedum-Trees Building | ST. LOUIS | International Life Building | SPOKANE | Peyton Building |
| MONTREAL | Merchants Bank Building | DETROIT | Ford Building | KANSAS CITY | Keith & Perry Building | PORTLAND, Ore., Northwestern Bank B'ldg |
| BALTIMORE | Continental Building | CLEVELAND | Hippodrome Building | OMAHA | Woodmen of the World Building | |

MINNEAPOLIS, Security Bank Bldg.    DALLAS, Southwestern Life Bldg.    SAN DIEGO, Spreckles Bldg.

# REWARD
# STOLEN JEWELRY

On Thursday night, June 24th, 1915, between the hours of 8:00 and 9:30 p. m., a private residence in Spokane, Wash., was entered and the following list of articles stolen:

One all platinum dinner ring, containing 41 diamonds, as per following description:

    1 diamond  weighing ½, 1-64 carats.
    2 diamonds weighting ½ less 6-64 carats.
    12 diamonds weighing 12-32 carats.
    6 diamonds weighing  6-50 carats.
    20 diamonds weighing 20-100 carats.
        All blue-white in color.
        Value, $350.00.

One solitaire diamond ring, Tiffany setting, 5-8ths and 1-16th carats.  Value, $110.00.

One 5-stone diamond ring, stock No. 8554 scratched inside, 90-100ths carat.  Value, $125.00.

One 3-stone diamond ring, stock No. 50085, weight about 1½ carats.  Value, $200.00.

One cluster diamond ring, set one stone in center surrounded by 6 small diamonds.  Value, $95.00.

THE FIDELITY & CASUALTY COMPANY OF NEW YORK offer a REWARD of fifteen (15%) per cent for the recovery of any portion of the above described jewelry.

*TO JEWELERS, PAWNBROKERS, PRECIOUS STONE DEALERS, ETC.:*

Should any of these articles be offered, endeavor to retain same, detain the person offering it, summon a police officer and show him this circular, then immediately notify the nearest of the above listed offices. Any reasonable advances will be paid.

TO POLICE OFFICIALS:

Officers detailed to search prisoners, examine pawnshops, etc., will please keep a close lookout and notify us immediately should any of the articles listed be recovered.

PINKERTON'S NATIONAL DETECTIVE AGENCY, *or its employees, under its rules, are not permitted to accept rewards.*

Any information imparted will be discreetly investigated and treated strictly confidential.

THIS REWARD expires July 1, 1916.

## Pinkerton's National Detective Agency
202 PEYTON BLDG., SPOKANE, WASH.

Telephone Main 234.                                            Spokane, July 15, 1915.

# STOLEN

From M. W. Trask's Hardware Store in Deer Lodge, on the night of March 10, 1912, the following described articles:

## KNIVES

200 Cattaraugus brand, with M. W. Trask on blade; 50 Boker Tree brand, 50 Case & Son brand, 25 Zenith brand.

## RAZORS

18 Cattaraugus Indian brand, 12 Zenith brand (Marshall Wells Hardware Co.), 1 Wade & Butcher, 2 Diamond Edge Safety, 2 Every Ready Safety, 1 Gillette Safety, 1 Auto Strop.

Arrest any person having any of the above articles and wire

## J. E. NEVILLE,

Sheriff of Powell County,
Deer Lodge, Montana.

# BANDIT BLOODIED BY BLAST 👉

With the two men standing so near the track, the motorman had few choices but to shut off the current and apply the breaks.

The Los Angeles Pacific daylight railcar rolled to a stop near Tokio Station and as easy as that the two masked bandits, Sam Barron and William Fox, climbed aboard. One entered the car from the front, the other from the rear, and together they meant business.

"Hands up everyone, and if anyone moves, I'll kill them," shouted one of the crooks.

He made his point firing three shots from his automatic pistol. The bullets tore into the roof of the railcar, prompting his overzealous partner to fire several blasts of his own, each skimming over the heads of the passengers.

These guys weren't fooling around. The first bandit ordered the conductor down the aisle to collect whatever loot the passengers carried. A second volley of warning shots blasted by the bandits hit young Harry Mitchell in the neck. The bullet then traveled on, crashing through a window and striking passenger Herbert Harlan in chest.

But Harlan's overcoat, undercoat and vest stopped the bullet in the nick of time. The man drew open his jacket, not to check his wound but to draw his revolver. Enraged, he fired point blank at Fox as the crook collected the loot from the passengers.

"The bullet struck the bandit in the side of his face, tearing out a number of teeth on both sides of his jaw," the *Los Angeles Examiner* reported. "The man staggered and fell but caught himself and ⌐d upright."

As Fox regained his balance, he fired his revolver in the direction of Harlan. "You'll try to shoot me up, will you?" the wounded Fox was reported to have screamed. "Why I'm the best shot in the country and you can't kill me."

With his jaw blown to bits, Fox lurched down the car, shouting at the conductor to continue taking money from the passengers while begging his buddy to get a move on. "Hurry up, Sam," Fox urged. "I'm shot and I can't hold out much longer."

Fox staggered down the aisle, growing ever dizzy, until he finally reached the rear door. The conductor's cap was full of loot—Fox grabbed it and then fell rather than jumped off the train. The last bandit was ready to abandon ship as well. But first, the motorman would have to give up his money and his ring.

The motorman complied but the bandit dropped the ring. When he stooped to pick it up, the motorman hit the current and the train lurched, knocking the bandit to the floor. It was a mistake. The bandit stood and shot the motorman, then jumped from the car, pausing long enough to empty his pistol. Glass crashed down on the terrified passengers and splintered wood flew about the cabin.

The alarm was given and the manhunt was on. A crook with half his jaw missing wouldn't be hard to find.

"We were in the neighborhood of Palms when a suspicious character with a bandage tied about the lower side of his face boarded the car," C. M. Daggett, the local constable, told reporters.

When the conductor went to collect the man's

# $500 REWARD

For arrest and conviction of Sam Barron, who on the night of January 25th, 1911, held up and robbed the passengers on the Los Angeles Pacific Railway car at Tokio Station, Ocean Park, Los Angeles County.

Sam Barron is described as follows:

Age about 30 years, height 5 ft. 9 or 10 inches, weight about 150 to 160 lbs., hair straw color, rather thin in front, eyes blue, nose has evidently been broken at some time and appears flat at the end, occupation teamster, cow puncher and general all around laborer, has worked on stock and cattle ranches in Montana and Dakota, claims to have been a soldier in South Africa during the Boer War, and also a sailor and takes great pride in relating his experiences during such service, in speech at times assumes a Southern accent, when last seen was wearing a black slouch hat, black sack coat, corduroy trousers, heavy lace shoes, was smooth shaven but can raise beard and mustache of a light reddish color. He will endeavor to obtain work in grading camps or on a ranch.

Take no chances with him as he has the reputation of being a gun man and will not hesitate to shoot.

The above reward is offered by the Los Angeles Pacific Railway Company, and as there is no question of a conviction, you will have no trouble in collecting the reward.

Wire all information to

## W. A. HAMMEL,
Sheriff of Los Angeles County

fare, the suspicious passenger said he had been kicked in the jaw by a mule. The conductor saw through the lie and, passing down the aisle, he winked at the constable. The two then met in the back of the train, certain the injured man was Fox.

"He told me that one of the bandits was on board and I decided to capture him," Daggett said.

"I threw open the door and told the bandit to throw up his hands, which he did."

Now, they just had to find the elusive Barron.

"Take no chances with him," the Los Angeles County sheriff warned his men. "He has the reputation of a gun man and will not hesitate to shoot."

# $50 REWARD
## For the Apprehension of
## JIM PAPPAS
### Alias Jim Korras, a Greek, for Robbery

He was arrested at Harrison May 16, 1915, and broke away from the officers at one o'clock that day and went into the wooded country between the Coeur d'Alene and St. Maries rivers, and is apt to try to cross one river or the other.

DESCRIPTION---About 26 to 30 years old, weight about 115 lbs., about 5 ft. 2 in. tall, black hair curly over temples, smooth shaven, beard about two days old when taken in custody, face rather thin or bony. He wore tan button shoes that had been half-soled and hobnailed, a striped suit of clothes between yellow and brown in shade, a very light colored soft shirt and black felt hat, did not have vest. He has round scar on chin near corner of mouth. Generally works on section or as short order cook.

If arrested notify us by wire, at our expense. We will pay a reward of $50.00 when he is turned over to us.

**T. L. QUARLES,**
COEUR D'ALENE, IDAHO
**Sheriff of Kootenai County**

RECEIVED
MAY 23 1915

*(Captured) Sent to Pen at Lodge*

# WANTED

*Escaped from Bozeman Oct /14*

# For Robbery

FRANK SHANNON.
4047.

## John Harrington,

### Alias Tige Harrington,
### Alias Frank Shannon,

Age 25 Years; Height 5 feet, 6 in.; Weight 135 lbs.; Eyes gray; Hair medium dark; Features boyish; Complexion medium dark

## ARREST AND WIRE AT MY EXPENSE.

## TIM DRISCOLL, Sheriff

**Silver Bow County** **BUTTE, MONTANA**

*Captured in Canada Sept /1910*

# $350 REWARD!
## FOR HOLD-UP MAN

One hundred dollars of above reward is offered by Jones & Co., of Harper, Oregon, for information that will lead to the arrest and conviction of the man who held up and robbed their store on the night of July 10, 1914.

The Post Office was robbed at the same time and the U. S. authorities offer from $50.00 to $250.00 reward in this kind of case. Lee Knight is the man wanted for this crime.

### Description

Lee Knight, whose real name is said to be Sam Shepherd, is a cowboy and rode in the sports here on the Fourth. He is also said to have ridden at Cheyenne and Pendleton. He generally wears a cowboy rig including long waisted corduroy pants with a belt. Down in front of these pants he always carries concealed, a long, blued barrel gun with which he is an expert shot. He prefers a blue suit when dressed up in which he makes a nice appearance. When in town he drinks considerable booze and sometimes talks quite freely. He works in the hay fields and makes a good hand.

He is about 25 years old, 5 feet 8 or 9 inches tall, weighs about 170 lbs., face full and red; brown hair; eyes blue, but change to brown when excited; gold tooth in front on upper jaw and is said to have other gold teeth in back of mouth. It seems certain that he has a large scar on one hand, where he was bitten by a horse, and that a finger or thumb is off at first joint.

Please send all information to

## D. H. KERFOOT, Sheriff.

Dated at Vale, Malheur County, Oregon, July 25th, 1914.                                    Card No. 3

Enterprise Print, Vale, Oregon

# ARREST FOR BANK ROBBERY.
## $200.00 REWARD.

The California Bankers Association will pay one hundred apiece for the arrest and conviction of the following described men; also ten per cent of all money recovered. There will be no trouble about the conviction. These two men, and one other who is under arrest, held up and robbed the Garden City Bank at Santa Clara, Cal., at noon, Sept. 3, 1919, and escaped with Four Thousand Five Hundred Dollars. *Eighteen Hundred of this is in ten and twenty dollar gold pieces.*

DESCRIPTION No. 1—**Mark Thornton** alias **"Shorty"** 5 ft. 6 or 7, 150 lbs.; brown hair, parted on side; smooth shaven; about 27 years old; nice looking; well dressed; wears pinch-back suit. Has old bullet wound in one of his wrists; very noticeable scar; wrist-bone sticks out from being set improperly.

DESCRIPTION No. 2 — **"Whitie"** or **"Swede" La Reeves**—5 ft. 8 or 9; 150 lbs.; light hair, combed straight back, pompadour; smooth shaven; about 25 years; pinch-back suits. Swedish appearance. Both have appearance of college men.

These men and two women, Viola Jeffries and Clara Thornton, left here on afternoon of September 3d, and were traced to Benecia, Calif., where they bought a ticket for Salt Lake, Utah. The women were arrested by Chief of Police at Los Angeles, September 9th. Claim they left men at Semloh Hotel, Salt Lake, Sunday afternoon, September 7th. This, I am certain, is true. They may go east, as Thornton's mother is supposed to live in New York City. He also has a girl, who lives in the suburbs of New York. He is well known in the East, and has served time in one of the eastern penitentiaries.

Show pictures to carnival and concession men. May have followed this line of work. La Reeves' home I am sure is in San Francisco. They may take jobs as bell hops for short while to cover up. Generally stop in rooming houses or hotels on edge of tenderloin district, but will spend their time in tenderloin or wherever there are cafes with entertainers. Joy riders. Will hire automobile and joy-ride to road-houses at every opportunity. Both can drive. Very successful with women of the night life and like to dance. Smoke Lucky Strike cigarettes; drink; will sniff hop whenever they can buy it. Don't look like hop-heads. If you have a stick-up job, look for these men. They have pulled stick-up jobs both night and day from one end of the Pacific Coast to the other, and have operated through the east at different times.

The above pictures are good likenesses. They were taken Aug. 30, 1919. La Reeves is left and Thornton, right. Both are armed. They carry their guns inside trousers at waist line in front. These men will stick together. Both of them have probably been in the U. S. Army. Thornton we know has. Any information as to what organization he belonged, or anything that will help this office to locate him, will be appreciated.

We hold felony warrant.

JACK BLACK,
Chief of Police,
San Jose, Cal.

GEORGE W. LYLE,
Sheriff Santa Clara County,
San Jose, Cal.

# OLD MAN ROUGHED UP AND ROBBED 👉

It wasn't a secret that the old man living on the edge of town held a distrust of banks. So when the citizens of Wolford, North Dakota, learned that burglars had broken into the man's home, beat him over the head, and made off with nearly $2,000 in cash, it didn't come as a big surprise.

"Old Man Beaten and Robbed," cried the headlines in the *Wolford Mirror*. "No Clue to the Robbers Discovered."

Sleeping in his home that night was E. E. Snyder, a deaf eighty-three-year-old man who had amassed quite a savings. But he didn't keep the money in a bank. Instead, he stored it in a wallet tucked under his pillow.

The crooks knew this and cut a hole in the screen of Snyder's home. Reaching through that hole they raised the hook. It was too easy. The two men were in, tiptoeing about with little fear of detection.

Upstairs that night slept Snyder's son and daughter-in-law. They heard nothing as the crooks stalked about like twin cats. The crooks disturbed nothing on their midnight prowl, except the double-barrel shotgun and the box of shells. Now it was time to go for the old man's cash.

"Mr. Snyder seemed to have a distrust for banks and it was common knowledge throughout this section that he always carried a considerable amount of ready money on his person," the paper reported.

Snyder stirred when the burglars grabbed him by the throat and began choking him. The old man put up a fight. Still, the crooks pounded him on the head until they knocked him unconscious.

With Snyder out like a light the burglars swiped his silver watch and fat wallet, the latter containing $1,665. Little did the crooks know that an equally impressive bounty would soon be placed upon their heads.

The robbers had slipped away before the son checked on his father. He found the man sitting on the edge of the bed in a terrible state. The old man's face was nearly "pounded to a pulp." He sat there like a child, crying that he had been robbed.

Sheriff Frank Rettinger and his deputy didn't waste any time responding to the call. They arrived at once and began their investigation, which included a countywide search for their suspect—an individual who had once worked for the old man during the harvest.

The sheriff knew exactly who he was after, that being one Howard Case, a thirty-four-year-old ex-soldier said to be a tough man. With tattoos on his forearm, gold teeth in his mouth, and a scar from a bullet wound, his appearance would be easy to peg.

The sheriff took no chances pursuing his suspect. He warned his deputies to be careful. He also noted that a $500 reward would be paid for the return of the old man's money "and the body of Howard Case."

News of the robbery was not a complete surprise, reported the *Wolford Mirror*. The only wonder expressed by the local residents was that the robbers didn't get more money from old man Snyder.

# $500 REWARD

## For Robbery and Assault

Howard Case, age 34 years, height 5 feet 10 inches, light complexion, slightly bald on top of head, tattooing on both forearms representing coat of arms, one gold tooth in upper jaw, probably two; has large vaccination mark on arm, scar on right thigh supposed to be caused by bullet; talks with slight southern accent, wears service fatigue or campaign hat mostly and had on red and black plaid stag shirt.

This man is suspected of breaking into a house at Wolford, N. D., on the night of August 23, 1916, choking and beating the owner into unconsiousness and robbing him of one Baker double barrel shotgun 12 gauge hammerless and one Elgin watch, open face, solid silver case, crystal nicked on edge also $1,665 mostly in bills of $20 and $50 denominations,

**The above reward of $500 will be paid for the return of $1500 or more, of the stolen money, and the body of Howard Case,**

This man is an ex-soldier and is a tough man. Officers are warned to take no chances when arresting him. Hold and wire at my expense.

FRANK RETTINGER, Sheriff,
Rugby, North Dakota

# Wanted For Burglary

### I Hold Warrant Charging Burglary
### for One

# GEORGE DUHL

### Age Twenty-eight or Thirty

Weight about 155 pounds; height about 5 feet 6 or 7 inches; eyes light; hair brown; complexion light; Dresses as lumberjack, medium high top shoes, hob-nailed; gray stag pants, dark blue coat.

Inveterate tobacco chewer but never smokes; is a drinking man. Claims to be structural iron worker.

## Has a birth mark on one side of his head covering part of ear and reaching well to the back of his head and down on his neck.

### If located, arrest, hold and wire at my expense.

---

## W. L. BROWN, Sheriff of Lincoln County
### LIBBY, MONTANA

June 20, 1917.

# $50. REWARD $50.

---

## Wanted for Embezzlement of $900.

### GEORGE W. FERRIS

Alias Montie Ferris, alias George Montie, alias Montie George, age 38 years, height 5 ft. 5 in., weight 145 pounds, dark complexion, dark hair parted in middle, smooth face, large nose, jewish features, front teeth gold from left to center, is a newspaper man, also worked as organizer for the Owls.

Arrest and wire any information at my expense.

FRANK A. GREEN,

Flint, Mich., July 10, 1913.                    Sheriff Genesee County

*This fellow is in Montana*

# $50 Reward

## For Embezzlement and Bond Jumping
## RODNEY DAVIS or W. R. DAVIS

### Alias Dick Jones or John Jones

American; about 42 or 44 years old, 5ft. 6in. high, blocky build, blue eyes, light hair and considerable bald, short thick neck; has bad rupture, shows thru pants.

Occupation: painter and paper hanger and belongs to Union; taking out card in Portland sometime last July or 1st of August; booze fighter, will get drunk if opportunity offers, worked at his trade part of September in steel ship yards of the Standiford Construction Co., Vancouver, Wash.

Officers, I want this man and want him bad; spare no expense. Wire, collect, all information to

## W. A. GOODMAN,

### Sheriff Harney County, Burns, Ore.

# Wanted For Embezzlement

## EDWARD R. COLLINS

### Defaulting Postmaster
### Goldfield, Nevada

This is a recent picture of Edward R. Collins, late Postmaster at Goldfield, Nevada, who is wanted for embezzlement of $5000 Government funds.

**Description.**—Age 43 years but appears younger; height 5 feet 7 inches; weight 160 to 170 pounds; hair light brown; eyes blue, large, prominent and piercing; lips quite thin and very close to teeth giving appearance of smiling at all times; ears are large and stand out from head; complexion dark and sallow. No. 16 collar; 8 or 8½ shoe; feet rather peculiarly shaped; wears frame glasses when reading and frequently when traveling; usually wears an Elk badge on lapel of coat, large diamond set Elk tooth watch charm; watch carried in upper vest pocket with small gold chain across chest to opposite vest pocket. He has on one limb above knee a scar caused by a 45-calibre bullet, this wound sometimes causes a slight limp; has a peculiar swing to his walk. Dresses neatly and always wears hat well down over the eyes. He smokes incessantly with cigar well in corner of mouth; chews tobacco which usually is carried in cloth receptacle in hip pocket; when standing habitually carries both hands in hip pockets. His conversation is rapid with frequent oaths. He is a butcher by trade but would hardly follow hard labor, more inclined to manipulate an investment of some kind.

Collins left Goldfield, Nevada, February 4, 1914, taking with him $5000 of Government funds. He was seen last in the vicinity of Los Angeles, Cal., February 12, 1914.

Warrant for his arrest is held by the United States Marshal. If located notify United States Marshal, Carson City, Nevada, and the undersigned.

### G. A. LEONARD,
Post Office Inspector in Charge,
San Francisco, California.

566

# Wanted --- C. W. Paul

Broke jail August 26, 1919, at Grangeville, Idaho
Charged with false pretenses

**Description:**       Age, 30 years; height, 6 feet 4 inches; weight, about 200 pounds; big hands; wears No. 12 shoes; complexion, light; blue eyes; light brown hair, combed back in big roach; rather good looking.   Will be wearing either brown suit of clothes, or brown corduroy pants, and brown woollen shirt; wears black hat.

Will be found around sporting women or pool halls. Has been arrested twice in Spokane, on vagrancy charge.  Claims to have been in the army or submarine service.

Please keep a sharp lookout for this man, if found, arrest, hold and wire.  Wire all information collect to

# W. H. ELLER

**Sheriff, Idaho county, Idaho            Grangeville, Idaho**

Please distribute this circular to all deputies and constables

# $50 REWARD

Escaped from an Officer by jumping off the train near Dillon, Montana, MANUAL LICIAZA, age about 27 years, height 5 feet 6 or 7 inches, weight 130 pounds; dark complexion, black hair, brown eyes and black mustache, and will probably be smooth shaven now; slim face, nose set slightly to the right side. When he left the train he had on a brown suit of clothes, pants had cuffs on the bottom, tan lace shoes, brown soft hat crushed in the middle. I hold a warrant charging Burglary for Liciaza. Occupation cook and is a dudish looking fellow; hangs around Mexicans or Spaniards; is a gambler and will be found around saloons and pool halls; talks plain and has a little Spanish accent.

JOHN KILLORN, Sheriff Park County.

Livingston, Montana.

# SHERIFF'S OFFICE
## BUTTE, MONTANA

On Monday, the 8th day of September, A. D. 1919, the South Side Bank at Butte, Montana, was held up by a lone bandit about the hour of 11:45 A. M.

He entered the Bank by a side door and made the employes crawl into the vault, which he closed, and then robbed the bank desk of the following described moneys:

ONE (1) $1000.00 Yellow Back United States Currency.

FORTY (40) Gold Twenties ($20.00).

FORTY (40) Gold Tens ($10.00).

$130.00 Gold Coins, Mixed Denominations. Amongst this gold were Two (2) Gold Twenties and Two (2) Gold Tens with the inscription "In God We Trust" omitted. These coins are very scarce and are at a premium by coin collectors.

$2700.00 in Currency of All Denominations, mostly Tens (10.00) and Twenties (20.00), with two or three $100.00 and $50.00 Bills amongst them. Some of this currency was wrapped with tape with South Side Bank or First National Bank of Butte name.

The bandit is described as follows:

Age, about 34; height, about 5 feet 10 or 11 inches; weight, about 160; complexion, light; hair, blonde (maybe dyed); eyes, blue; was wearing dark suit (probably gray); grayish-brown Fedora hat; square-toed shoes, and amber goggles.

Wire any information to

JOHN K. O'ROURKE, Sheriff.

Butte, Montana.

# THE DAYLIGHT ROBBERY

At high noon and in broad daylight a lone bandit ducked into the South Side Bank in Butte, Montana, and ordered the cashier and his assistant to crawl into the vault.

"And be quick about it," the crook said.

The bandit told the cashier's assistant to open the safe. The poor man trembled with fear and did his best to comply. But he couldn't complete the combination, and the robber groaned in dismay.

It was taking too long. Running out of options the bandit locked the two men into the vault, thus gaining unfettered access to the $5,000 available elsewhere in the bank.

With the money now in hand, the robber slipped away. All he left behind was a single rumor that said he wore amber auto-goggles and a fedora.

It wasn't much to go on. But police combed the city's streets looking for the slick city bandit. Uptown, midtown, downtown—officers found nothing.

Yet reports from the sheriff's office came down the line. The crook was seen motoring toward the eighteen-mile hill. Silver Bow Sheriff John O'Rourke was in hot pursuit.

O'Rourke's deputies were confident they'd make an arrest by day's end. Meanwhile, the bank's president found himself promising his patrons that their losses were covered by insurance.

The citizens of Butte didn't likely care, as *Oh Baby* was coming to town, complete with its "peaches" of beauty—peaches that promised to perform in an area mine for a pre-show matinee. "The chicklets probably will interrupt the work to some extent, but according to eastern critics, they are a sight for sore eyes," the ad read.

O'Rourke had no time for chicklets and Broadway shows. Dancing girls were the last thing on his mind, peaches or not. He'd failed to catch the South Side robber and knew against his other wishes that he probably never would.

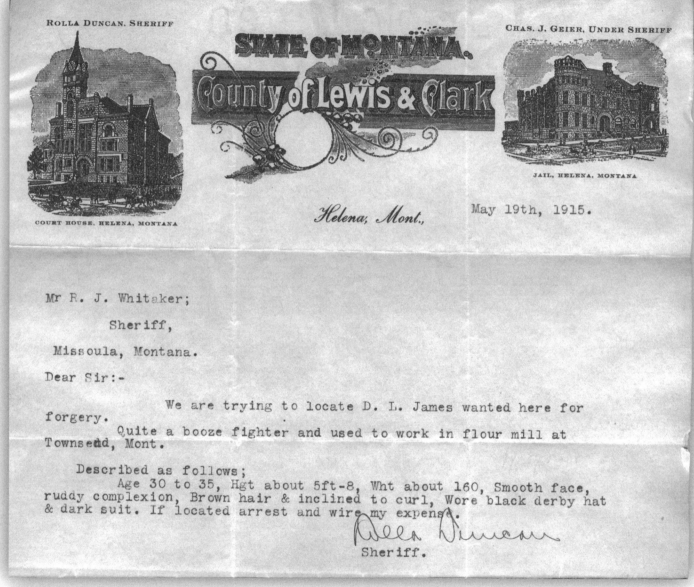

ROLLA DUNCAN, SHERIFF

CHAS. J. GEIER, UNDER SHERIFF

STATE OF MONTANA.
County of Lewis & Clark

COURT HOUSE, HELENA, MONTANA

JAIL, HELENA, MONTANA

Helena, Mont.,          May 19th, 1915.

Mr R. J. Whitaker;

        Sheriff,

    Missoula, Montana.

Dear Sir:-

            We are trying to locate D. L. James wanted here for
forgery.
            Quite a booze fighter and used to work in flour mill at
Townsend, Mont.

    Described as follows;
            Age 30 to 35, Hgt about 5ft-8, Wht about 160, Smooth face,
ruddy complexion, Brown hair & inclined to curl, Wore black derby hat
& dark suit. If located arrest and wire my expense.

                                        Rolla Duncan
                                        Sheriff.

# WANTED, FOR FORGERY

++++++++++++++

Wanted, for Forgery, committed at Goldendale, Wash., May 24, 1913: HARRY MAYS, alias Jack Harbin; aged about 30 years; height about 5 feet 6 inches; weight about 145 to 150 pounds; smooth shaven; dark hair; dark eyes; medium light complexion; cheeks somewhat hollow; tatoo on left fore arm containing the letters H. M. When last seen wore a brown coat, dark striped pants, a blue shirt and a soft dark hat, but no vest. Is a painter of buildings and vehicles and is supposed to carry a putty knife and possibly a paint brush or so.

IS A BOOZER, A DOPE FIEND AND AN ALL-AROUND DEAD-BEAT

Is known to have knocked around under various names and has been in jail in different places. Arrest, hold and notify me at my expense. I hold warrant and want him badly and he is sure to turn a bad trick somewhere else.

F. A. SMITH, Sheriff of Klickitat County,
Dated May 27, 1913　　　　　　　Goldendale, Washington

# WANTED FOR FORGERY

Man about 40 years old, square jawed; has German accent. About 5 feet 7 or 8 inches tall, stocky build, smooth shaven when last seen on November 24. Weight about 175. Think eyes are dark; hair dark, probably streaked with gray. When last seen wore a loose fitting salt and pepper over-coat and high crowned black crusher hat, fedora. Has quiet, unassuming, dignified manner. Favorite drink is gin rickey.

Posed here as manufacturer of varnish and gave name of George Hilger, of Cleveland, O. Will probably change name. Gave check on special printed form of Glidden Varnish Company, drawn on Seaboard National Bank of New York. Pretended to be in the market for farm and city property. Probably wanted at other places.

If apprehended hold and notify

## W. H. GEBO Sheriff

### Red Lodge, Carbon County, Montana

December 3, 1915.

Journal

# $25.00 REWARD
# FOR ARREST

Circular No._____

### SHERIFF'S OFFICE,
#### Dillon, Montana, July 10, 1911.

# WANTED FOR FORGERY
# A. E. ROBINSON

## DESCRIPTION:

Age, about 45 years; height, 5 feet 10 inches; weight, 160 pounds; light complexion; brown hair; sandy moustache; rather sharp face; some teeth out in front; a little stoop shouldered; occupation, sheep herder; has herded in Montana for a long time; while in a conversation he continuously uses the words "gemny Christmas."

This man forged a check in Dillon, Mont., on the third day of July, 1911, and left here the next day.

We have no trace of which way he went.

If located, arrest, hold and wire at my expense. I hold warrant.

## O. C. GOSMAN, Sheriff,
## Dillon, Montana.

# THE TEXAS SWINDLER

He was the president of a large business. She was his secretary and lover. Together they became felons wanted for forgery and swindling.

A. B. Crouch and his thirty-five-year-old private secretary, Mrs. Buchanan, duped the town of Temple, Texas, out of an untold sum of money by ensuring the failure of the Crouch Grain Company.

Those left counting their financial losses included a Wichita Falls elevator operation whose order of thirty prepaid grain cars was diverted and sold. Adding to the scandal was the fact that Crouch was a married man, and married men should steer clear of their private secretaries.

"Mrs. Crouch is prostrated," the *Temple Telegram* declared. "Her condition is said to be worsening."

The entire town of Temple had fallen victim to the scandal. Even the newspaper reporter rang in on the matter, sacrificing the integrity of his story to allow Chase Campbell, president of the City National Bank, a chance to editorialize on the crime.

"There has been entirely too much fuss over the whole affair—a great deal more talk and excitement than the losses involved justify," Campbell said.

Campbell never bothered to mention exactly what the losses were, other than to say that they would be "much smaller than the street rumors have it." Campbell did his best to convince the public that the bank's losses were scattered between "so many" ventures that the difference would hardly be noticed.

But there was still the matter of Crouch's whereabouts. Would the businessman ever make good on the money? Campbell thought so, going out on a limb to suggest that when Crouch was located he could be convinced he had nothing to run from in the first place.

"When he returns, the City National will stand ready to cooperate with his other friends in getting him re-established here," Campbell said. "Crouch has been one of the most successful businessmen in the county, and it would be a misfortune for a temporary business reverse to wreck his life."

But one couldn't help but believe that Campbell's use of the *Temple Telegram* was an underhanded ploy to lure Crouch back to town for collection and prosecution.

"He is still young," Campbell said, praising Crouch the swindler at every turn. "His life is before him. He has ability, energy, and ambition. This bank has stood by him and enabled him to make money in the past, and with the cooperation of his other friends, it stands ready to do so again."

While Campbell praised Crouch for his ambition, police circulated wanted posters offering a reward of $500 for the arrest of the man and his secretary.

# Temple Texas, Mar. 27, 1916
# Reward $500.00

MRS. BUCHANAN

A. B. CROUCH             A. B. CROUCH

The following rewards will be paid for the arrest and delivery to Sheriff of Bell county in any jail in the United States, Canada, or any foreign port: $250.00 EACH—$250.00 EACH.

A. B. Crouch and Mrs. Buchanan are wanted for forgery and felony swindling at Temple, Texas.

### A. B. CROUCH IS DESCRIBED AS FOLLOWS:

Age—36 years.

Height—5 feet 10 or 11 inches.

Weight—155 or 160 pounds.

Complexion—Fair.

Eyes—Blue.

Hair—Light brown.

Dress—Plain and neat.

Occupation—Grain dealer.

Peculiarities—Neither smokes or chews tobacco

### MRS. BUCHANAN IS DESCRIBED AS FOLLOWS:

Age—35 years.

Height—5 feet 5 or 6 inches.

Weight—110 or 115 pounds.

Build—Slender.

Complexion—Sallow.

The above is a specimen of Crouch's handwriting in check form.

Signed

# HUGH SMITH

Sheriff, Bell County, Texas.

# WANTED!
## FOR FORGERY

# A. E. Bramwell
### Alias A. E. Bornwell    Alias L. H. Hamilton

Age, 35 yrs.; Height, 5 ft. 8 1-2 in.; Weight,
160 lbs.; Complexion, Sallow; Hair, Yellow
Nationality, Swedish;   Occupation,  Steel
Granary  Worker;  Teeth Noticeably Black
Some Gold on Upper Front Teeth
Slightly Hump Shouldered

## I Hold Warrant Charging Forgery
## Arrest and Notify

*A. E. Bramwell*
*Bornwell - alias*
*L. H. Hamilton*

# Del E. Gray
### Sheriff

**Bozeman, Mont., Sept. 9, '15**

Daily Chronicle Print

# WANTED
## FOR FORGERY

JOE LANPADA and also a woman traveling as his wife. LANPADA is an Italian, thirty years of age, black wavy hair, broad shoulders, well-dressed, very dark skin, red cheeks, about 5 feet, 6 inches tall. His wife is an American, tall, blond, very prominent scar extending from lip to chin.

These parties left Miles City on or about April 1st, checking three trunks from Forsyth west over the Chicago, Milwaukee and Puget Sound Railway Company's line.

Arrest and Notify:  BEN LEVALLEY,
Miles City, Mont., April 14, 1911   Sheriff of Custer Co.

Ingham, Printer, Miles City, Montana

# $25.00 REWARD
## FOR ARREST

Circular No. 1

**SHERIFF'S OFFICE,**
Dillon, Mont., July 10, 1911.

# WANTED FOR FORGERY
# F. Madden, alias Frank Moore
## DESCRIPTION:

Age, about 35 years; height, 6 feet; weight, 165 pounds; rather raw boned; medium light complexion; blue eyes and cross eyed; light brown hair; has large nose; good teeth; smooth face; ranch hand by occupation; walks a little pigeon toed; is a little stooped shouldered. At the time he left here he was wearing soft black slouch hat, blue overalls, dark coat and vest. Left here July 15, 1911.

If located, arrest, hold and wire at my expense. I hold warrant.

O. C. GOSMAN, Sheriff,
Dillon, Montana.

# WANTED--For Forgery
# Wm. H. WHITE

DESCRIPTION---Height. about 5 feet, 10 inches; weight about 180 lbs., hair, brown; little curly and thin in center in front; eyes, blue, mustache, dark brown but may be smooth shaven now; upper front teeth bad when last seen; small cancer under one shoulder blade; generally well dressed; wears 8 1-2 shoe; heavy drinker when in town; chews tobacco and smokes a pipe; talks low; has a brother working for the C. M. & P. S. Ry. as a fireman out of Marmarth, N. D.; his old home is at Marian, Iowa, and his parents still live there.

I hold warrant of arrest. If found arrest and notify,
BEN LEVALLEY, Sheriff,
Miles City, Montana

OFFICE OF

# Sheriff of Blaine County

*Hailey, Idaho* JANY 25th, 1914.

WANTED FOR GRAND LARCENY.

JACK RILEY,-Age about 35,height-about 5ft 9 in,
weight about 175,-dark hair rather bald in front,
sandy beard,smooth shaven,-Irishman very talkative
and has habit of saying "YAH" quite often and rather laud.

Was a rancher here,and run a butcher shop in Montana before coming here,is a good worker.

This man Riley is wanted here for cattle rustling,
Arrest hold and wire at my expense.I hold warrant.

       Aaron Clements,Sheriff Blaine County,

          Hailey Idaho.

# WANTED

## For Forgery

Charles B. Kennedy, last seen at Stevensville, about 5 feet 8 inches tall, brown hair, closely cropped sandy mustache, brown eyes, flushed face, about 45 years old, left hand withered, but can use thumb and forefinger, wearing dark brown or tan shoes with broad toe, brown hat of Columbian shape, black suit with light stripe, soft shirt with military colar. He drinks a good deal. We hold warrant. When located, arrest him and wire

# B. S. CHAFFIN, Sheriff

## Hamilton, Montana

Ravalli Republican, Printers

# THE SAFE-BLOWERS 👉

It was a hot night in the old Wyoming town when the two men set the charge and stepped back to watch it blow.

With a bang, the safe cracked and the loot inside was as good as theirs. Nothing could stop them from dashing off with what papers called the largest haul in northern Wyoming.

The alarm rang out when the sun rose over the dusty streets. It didn't take investigators long to reason that the burglars had gained access to the Monarch Trading Company through a back window some time during the night. Because the store clerks locked up at 11:00 p.m., investigators were certain that the crime had taken place after the midnight hour. Now it was time to tally the losses and give chase.

"Part of the money belongs to Uncle Sam," the headlines declared.

The great uncle wanted his money back. But the crooks were pros and wouldn't be an easy catch. Despite the hour in which the crime took place, no one in the neighborhood heard the crooks blow the safe.

"So far, no trace of the men has been made," the *Sheridan Post* read. "It is believed, though, that their identity has been fixed and descriptions of them secured."

The local sheriff wasted no time circulating fliers. Descriptions of the two men hit the streets. One was good looking but short and portly, weighing almost 200 pounds. The other held a "sunburned or rough looking" appearance.

A reward of $200 each wasn't too much to pay considering what the thieves had scored in their late-night haul. The duo made off with a healthy catch that included $574 in stamps, $447 in cash, $163 in store coupons, and 600 blank money orders.

Any man found in possession of the loot would have to answer to directly to the sheriff, and one angry uncle.

# The Post Office Department

Offers

# $200.00
# REWARD

For Each of the Men Who Blew Open the SAFE and Robbed the POST OFFICE at

# Monarch, Wyoming,

the Night of AUGUST 1st, 1916, when the following described property was STOLEN:

**$574.86 in Stamps; $447.71 in Money; 600 Blank Postal Money Orders, numbered 11601 to 12200, inclusive; $163.00 in Monarch Trading Co. Coupons**

The men thought to have committed this crime described as follows:
One, about 5 ft. 8 or 9 in. tall, Weight about 190 lbs, Grayish hair rather good looking and portly; Wore dark grey suit, light straw or Panama hat; Carried a small brown grip.

The other, Weight about 180 lbs, Square build, Brown hair, Medium height, Sunburned or rough looking; Wore dark suit.

Arrest and hold anyone found in possession of any of the above described property and wire me at my expense.

# O. MOSSBERG, Sheriff
# SHERIDAN, WYOMING

UNION LABEL

# Wanted for Grand Larceny

---

Man giving name Professor Warn, who operated here as Clairvoyant, Magnetic Healer and Chiropractor.

DESCRIPTION: APPEARS TO BE FORTY-FIVE YEARS; EYES ARE DARK BLUE; EYEBROWS ARE BLACK AND HEAVY; HAIR BLACK, LONG IN FRONT, PARTS ON SIDE, THROWN BACK, FEW GRAY HAIRS; RATHER HEAVY CHIN; HAS WHAT IS CALLED A LONG FACE; COMPLEXION DARK; WEIGHT ABOUT 155; HEIGHT ABOUT 5 FEET, 8 INCHES; SLIM BUILD; HAS GOLD IN TEETH; HANDS AND FINGERS SHORT; STEPS SHORT AND QUICK; MAKES GOOD APPEARANCE, ALTHOUGH EDUCATION IS LIMITED; GOOD TALKER, SMILING OFTEN WHEN TALKING; HAS SOME TATTOOING ON RIGHT FOREARM, I THINK; LAUNDRY MARK B-7-9.

This man plays the old game of deception. He induced a woman here to give him $535 (as much as she could raise) which he placed in an envelope to be magnetized, after a stated time. Upon opening the envelope she found worthless paper instead of currncy she had placed there, Professor Warn having disappeared meanwhile.

Please scrutinize all men operating along any lines of this kind; if found arrest, and wire any information to

ED RAND, Sheriff,

## Baker, Oregon

September 29th, 1913.

# DAY LETTER
## CONTINENTAL TELEGRAPH COMPANY
### INCORPORATED

This Company **TRANSMITS** and **DELIVERS** messages only on conditions limiting its liability, which have been assented to by the sender of the following **Day Letter.**

Errors can be guarded against only by repeating a message back to the sending station for comparison, and the Company will not hold itself liable for errors or delays in transmission or delivery of **Unrepeated Day Letters**, sent at reduced rates, beyond a sum equal to ten times the amount paid for transmission; nor in any case beyond the sum of **Fifty Dollars**, at which, unless otherwise stated below, this message has been valued by the sender thereof, nor in any case where the claim is not presented in writing within sixty days after the message is filed with the Company for transmission.

This is an **UNREPEATED DAY LETTER**, and is delivered by request of the sender, under the conditions named above.

**U. J. FRY, Superintendent.**

Un Co Mo 50 Blue

RECEIVED AT

Falcon Ida May 22

*Apprehended in Msla.*
*May 23/16.*

Hugh Kelly

    Sheriff Missoula, Mont.

Arrest Search and Hold Chas Dagget Barber Slender about 5 ft

8 inches high Large teeth thin face dark clothes soft black

hat thirty years old passenger today on CM & StP train

eighteen Avery to Missoula hold on suspicion and I will

arrive on train sixteen reference  D V Stephenson .
                  Walter F Belcher

313Pm

*Recd. at 6 30 P.M.*

# $25 REWARD

FOR THE ARREST OF

# EARNEST FREE

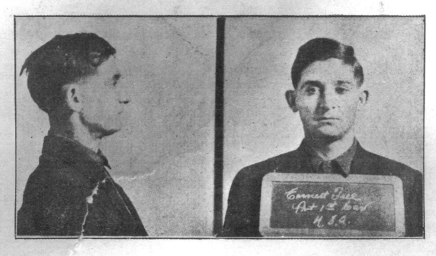

Finger-print classification: $\dfrac{1\ U}{1\ Ua}$ 5

## CHARGED WITH GRAND LARCENY

**DESCRIPTION:** White; born in Burnett, Tex.; age, 26 years; occupation, barber, blacksmith, mule-skinner, brakeman on railroad; registered in draft at Great Falls, Mont.; eyes, blue; hair, dark brown; complexion, dark; height, 5 feet 9½ inches; weight, 159 pounds. Prominent scars and marks: Front view — scar near center of forehead, on nose, and left knee. Back view — scar on left index finger.

A reward of $25.00 is payable for the apprehension of this man. Any information that may be secured as to the whereabouts of this man should be communicated to

**LESLIE McCANN, Stock Inspector, or J. H. STEPHENS, Sheriff**

**LEWISTOWN, MONT.**

June 21, 1918.                     25416

UNION LABEL  Fergus County Democrat, Inc.

# WANTED
## FOR GRAND LARCENY

At Three Forks, Montana, August 20th, 1913, **W. A. Cunningham.** Description as follows: Age about 45 or 50; height about five feet seven or eight inches; eyes gray; bald on top of head; hair dark, streaked with gray; wore dark slouch hat; brown suit of clothes; smooth shaven; powder burn or scar under left eye; leans forward when walking.

This man poses as a land buyer, and his stunt is to deposit worthless checks or drafts in a bank and then check on same.

If apprehended, arrest and wire at my expense. I hold warrant.

## W. S. EVANS,
### Sheriff Gallatin County, Bozeman, Montana

# ARREST THIS MAN FOR GRAND LARCENY

## Warrant in Sheriff's Office at San Bernardino, Cal.

# $500 $500

# Reward Reward

### ORRIS O. BUDD alias ORA BUDD

DESCRIPTION:—ORRIS O. BUDD, alias ORA BUDD, American; Age 36; Height, about 6 feet 2 inches; Weight, about 170 pounds; Slender Build, Bony Frame; Hair, dark, thick and rather curley, and slightly mixed with grey; Brown Eyes; Sallow complexion; (1) Gold Tooth upper right side, Teeth on upper right side crowded close together; Slender features and prominent Nose. Is an Ice Cream and Candy maker by trade, but has worked at mining for the last 3 or 4 years. Sometimes he wears an Elks pin, was a member of the Elks Lodge at Springfield, Ill. On August 2nd, 1913, at San Bernardino, Cal., a Felony Warrant was issued for this man, for Grand Larceny, charging him with the Theft of $5500.00 worth of Diamonds. This Agency will pay $500.00 Reward for the Arrest and Detention of this man until an Officer from the Sheriff's Office of San Bernardino, California, can reach him with the proper papers. We will go any where to get and extradite this man. The above picture was taken about 4 years ago, but is a good picture of him today.

### CITIZEN'S DETECTIVE AGENCY
#### H. J. RAYMOND, Manager

Wire all Information to J. G. RALPHS, Sheriff, San Bernardino County, San Bernardino, Cal., or CITIZEN'S DETECTIVE AGENCY, H. J. RAYMOND, Manager, Los Angeles, Cal.

# BIBLIOGRAPHY/CITATIONS

Jerry Adams, "Texas Outlaw Sam Bass's Coin," Trade Token Tales, www.members.fortunecity.com/token guy/tokentales/page50.htm

Ronald H. Beights, *Jesse James and The First Missouri Train Robbery* (Pelican, 2002).

Butch Cassidy and the Outlaw Trail on KUED-7, www.kued.org

James H. Earle, ed., *The Capture of Billy the Kid* (College Station, TX. Creative Publishing, 1988).

Jack Epstein, "Butch Cassidy, Sundance Kid Found a Haven in Argentine," *Christian Science Monitor*, Jan. 27, 1998, www.csmonitor.com

Barbara Fifer, *Montana's Mining Ghost Towns* (Farcountry Press, 2002).

L. R. Kirchner, *Robbing Banks: An American History, 1831-1999* (Rickville Centre, NY: Sarpedon, 2000).

Saint Louis Iron Mountain and Pacific Railway, Jackson, MO, "Jesse James—The Show-Me State's Most Famous Train Robber," www.rosecity.net/trains/james_gang. html

Securitas Services USA, Inc., www.pinkertons.com

Union Pacific Railroad Museum, www.uprr.com/history/museum

Wells Fargo Online, www.wellsfargo.com

Western Outlaw Lawman Association, www.westernoutlaw.com

Wyoming Trails and Tales, www.wyomingtrailsandtales.com

## ARIZONA
"A Father's Vengeance," p. 102
*Verde Copper News*, July, 8, 1915

## CALIFORNIA
"Bandit Bloodied by Blast," p. 170
*Los Angeles Examiner*, January 26, 1911

"Cold-Blooded Killers," p. 58
*Lake County Bee*, May 8, 1914

"The Killer with Poor Manners," p. 67
*Press Democrat*, March 2, 1915

"Promise of Marriage," p. 108
*Contra Costa Gazette*, February 25, 1911

"Rail Robbers Escape Gunfire," p. 150
*Los Angeles Examiner*, June 12, 1915

"Rotting Body Launches Manhunt," p. 70
*Visalia Daily Chronicle*, February 23, 1916

"Safe-Blowers and Shooters," p. 95
*Sacramento Bee*, August 29, 1914;
September 1, 1914

## COLORADO
"A Dark Night at Utah Junction," p. 73
*Rocky Mountain News*, November 21–24, 28, 30, 1912; December 1, 2, 5, 12, 15, 16, 1912

"Deadly Gunfight at Colorado Station," p. 79
*Colorado Springs Gazette*, September 14–19, 1918; November 20, 1918

## IDAHO
"The Axe Killer," p. 76
*Teton Peak Chronicle*, May 11, 1916

"Spring Fever," p. 116
*Shoshone Journal*, March 28, 1919

## MONTANA
"The Apple-Picking Killer," p. 56
*Silver State Post*, September 13, 20, 1911;
November 15, 1911

"The Daylight Robbery," p. 185
*Butte Miner*, September 14, 1919

"The Man Who Wouldn't Die," p. 154
*Daily Missoulian*, March 18, 19, 1916

"Murder on a Farm," p. 82
*Western News*, August 3, 1911

## NORTH DAKOTA
"Old Man Roughed Up and Robbed," p. 176
*The Wolford Mirror*, August 24, 1916

## NEVADA
"The Quietest Thief," p. 161
*Tonopah Daily Bonanza*, March 14, 1912

## TEXAS
"Smooth Talker Walks Free," p. 123
*Wichita Daily Times*, January 5, 1915

"The Texas Swindler," p. 190
*Temple Telegram*, March 16, 1916

## UTAH
"Murder for Revenge," p. 63
*Salt Lake Tribune*, January 11, 12, 14–16, 19, 1914

## WASHINGTON
"Betrayed," p. 89
*Ellensburg Record*, August 5, 1913

Great Northern Terror, p. 86
*Yakima Daily Republic*, February 21, 1914

"The Jail Break," p. 134
*Tacoma Times*, January 4, 5, 6, 7, 11, 1918

"Who Shot Sheriff Scott?" p. 96
*Seattle Daily Times*, April 8, 1920

## WYOMING
"Crazed Wyoming Shooter," p. 90
*Rawlins Republican*, January 23, 1919

"The Safe-Blowers," p. 198
*Sheridan Post*, August 4, 1916

"A Shepherd's Revenge," p. 92
*Rawlins Republican*, August 24, 31, 1916

"Wyoming Jail Break," p. 140
*Sheridan Post*, August 19, 22, 26, 29, 1913

**Barbara Fifer** is an editor and writer who freelances from Helena, Montana. She wrote the history sections of *Along the Trail with Lewis and Clark* (Farcountry Press, 2nd ed., 2002) and is sole author of *Going Along with Lewis and Clark* (American & World Geographic, 2000), *Wyoming's Historic Forts* (Farcountry Press, 2002), *Montana's Mining Frontier Ghost Towns* (Farcountry Press, 2002), *Day-by-Day with Lewis and Clark* (Farcountry Press, 2003), *Lewis and Clark Expedition Illustrated Glossary* (Farcountry Press, 2003), and *EveryDay Geography of the United States* (GuildAmerica Books, Doubleday Direct, Inc., 2000).

**Martin Kidston** is a graduate of the University of Montana in Missoula. He now freelances from his home in Helena, Montana, and writes for the *Independent Record*, covering outdoor, feature, and general assignment stories. His work has appeared in various publications, including the *Washington Post* and *Montana Magazine*.